The World of Work

Introduction

Since I started writing   past
experiences as a child, as a car owner and as a
restorer of a house in a foreign land. I have so far
ignored one of the most common experiences for all in
a 'foreign land' - going to work.
Unless you are fortunate enough to be an internet or
social media billionaire and create your work
environment to suit you, most of us are forced to
inhabit an environment at work not of our own making
and usually not as we would ideally like it to be. Work
gives you the opportunity to interact with other
humans outside your immediate circle of family or
chosen friends. Sometimes this means being thrown
together with people that you would normally, given a
free choice, run away screaming from. But it also may
provide the opportunity to meet and interact with new,
pleasant people you wouldn't normally meet and this
can often be an enriching experience.

I hope to provide some insights that I have gained
through my years at work to help others through the
experience. Some of the advice will be contradictory -
the world is full of contradictions, so don't blame me! I
am also now of an age when looking back and reliving
the past through writing is an enjoyable experience
and according to medical experts is also helpful for the
health of those of us of advanced age. Most of my
working life took place in the latter half of the
twentieth century but the experiences are universal
and mostly based around human interactions.

When I first retired there were a number of occasions
when groups of ex-colleagues would meet up over a
lunch or supper and this was always an enlightening
experience. It was like two separate tribes meeting on
common ground for the first time with neither of them

able to see the other's perspective. Those people still at work would broadcast in great detail the corporate ins and outs of latest company goings on - who was doing what, who was promoted, what the latest shiny corporate initiatives and edicts were, with varying degrees of enthusiasm or cynicism. The retired people would feign interest with varying degrees of success depending on their acting skills whilst at the same time answering questions that now seemed irrelevant to them such as "but what do you find to do all day?" Once the rubicon of escape from the organisation had been crossed it was as if a veil had been lifted - 'How did all this company rubbish seem so important ?" The sad truth is that when you are inside any organisation you have to take it seriously or you would go mad. It's like looking behind the curtain in "The Wizard of Oz." The fallacy of the Great OZ can't be exposed.

So how to survive and remain sane?

First of all, I am not entirely confident that I am the right person to advise on work. The reason for this could be explained in the answer I would give to people early on in my retirement. They would ask -"So how are you finding retirement - do you miss work?" And I would answer -"Well I seem to have adapted quite well as the years of work seemed to have been an unnatural state between being a student and being retired, both of which seem to suit me rather better." Of course the compensation with work is that you receive financial reward which along with the opportunities for cheap entertainment seem to be the two most significant reasons for persevering with it. There is one overriding lesson that I have learned and that is it is absolutely essential to 'be yourself' at work and that to do anything else is a recipe for all sorts of stresses and unnecessary strains that people put on themselves. I always find it upsetting and rather sad when meeting or hearing about someone who is

2

deadly serious and boring at work being described as "not like that away from work - they are much more human and relaxed with friends away from work!"
The other apparent benefit of work is the social aspect of mixing with other humans as we are often told that we are social or tribal animals. I would contend that we are all tribal but to a greater or lesser degree. I can remember my first day at school being asked whether I knew any others in the class and when I answered positively by pointing to a larger child from our road that our mothers had once organised a 'play afternoon' together; but when the teacher asked whether I would like to sit next to him I swiftly answered "no thank you." So I started my education sitting, happily, in a double desk so maybe I am not a very social animal after all.

Given that the average person will spend a significant proportion of their life 'at work,' the adoption of a different persona would seem to me to be an unnecessary mental strain and not to be recommended.
I am also aware that the working environment is constantly changing and that the recent post-pandemic world is wrestling with WFH (working from home), either totally or in hybrid forms and this is creating new dilemmas for organisations and individuals.
So, what have I learned about work ?
To answer this I need to take myself back through my experiences at work, I know I will enjoy this process and maybe it will also echo to others.

Before I do this I would like to record what I think are my strongest lessons learnt in my career in the hope it may help somebody, even a little.

The cliche 'you work to live, not vice versa' is true for most. A successful career is not a success if it ruins your personal life.

Work takes a huge chunk of your time and you must find enjoyment in at least some of it. If you don't then you are definitely in an unsuitable job for you and need to find something else.

Don't fear change - it will happen anyway and you will gain greater control if you initiate some change yourself and learn not to feel great anxiety from it.

Give everyone a hearing - you will learn something, even from idiots.

Be yourself - it's hard to keep up the pretence of being something you are not - it's the road to stress and madness.

Doing new stuff which may be a little scary at first is better than the boredom of doing the same old stuff.

Perfection is an illusion and not usually attainable - just in time good enough is achievable.

One of the most important realisations for me was about an organisation. An organisation has a character and a culture but it comprises people. To achieve things and get things done you have to engage with, influence, persuade and convince those people about your ideas or project. I concluded quite early on (and it sounds like a cliche) that people skills are more important than technical skills.

So what happened during my working life?

As a child in the 1950's and 60's work was where my Dad went off to every day, apart from weekends and holidays. One of my earliest memories was walking with my Mum together with my younger brother in a push chair to meet my Dad from work. Given the distance, at least two miles, a walk down from our Swansea home in the suburb of Tycoch, through Singleton Park and probably along some of the beach and promenade, until we would wait for my Dad on the Strand which bordered the River Tawe. Dad worked in the offices of Unit Superheaters who manufactured large pipes for use in pressurised boilers but I knew nothing of this. All I knew was that a certain time, probably five o'clock the gates would open and what seemed like hundreds of men and a few women would all swarm through and we would try and spot my Dad and we would wave to each other before all going together into town to catch the bus home.

School Jobs

My own first job was similar to many - a paper round. I guess I was around fourteen and I had heard from friends that having a paper round gave the opportunity to supplement your pocket money and was something that only took half an hour or so in the morning or evening and would earn you at least twice as much as your weekly pocket money and maybe more. At the time my demands on my finances were mostly made by my hobbies of the time, mainly fishing, photography, buying records and Scouts and it was the last of these that probably tipped the balance in favour of employment. I didn't mind getting up early and my hobby of fishing had probably contributed to this as at weekends I met friends early on a Saturday to go fishing. There was a theory, not substantially proven to my mind, that fish were more likely to be caught in the early morning. The same theory also suggested dusk was a good time, leading to us sometimes arriving home late for our evening meal after having 'one last cast, for the big one.'

No, it was scouts that were placing a demand on my finances as the annual summer camps had increasingly got more ambitious, graduating from camp-sites in mid Wales to a trip the previous year to Southern Ireland, in County Cork and my first holiday outside England and Wales. The following summer the camp was even more ambitious - a mainland European trip on the Continent! We were to travel in our own coach to Belgium, Luxembourg, Germany and Holland over a fortnight. My parents offered to pay for the trip but we agreed that I would have to supply my own spending money and not being a great saver it was clear that I needed to raise money over and above my pocket money. So the paper round it was. I think it was a learning experience, waking to an alarm clock and going out before school, whatever the weather. Also hearing the newsagent grumbling when other

6

paperboys didn't turn up and learning an early lesson about the benefits of being reliable. I didn't mind it when the mornings were bright and dry but the wet mornings were less appealing. Nevertheless, I raised the spending money for the camp which I guess my parents probably added to. The camp was a great success and quite different from normal camps. The simpler and more rustic pleasures of these are covered in my earlier book (A 1950's Boy - available from Amazon.)

It was more of a European sight seeing tour, mostly using city campsites with better facilities such as shower blocks and on-site shops and cafes, not the rustic camps we had previously experienced. There was the revelation that beer and lager could be bought by fourteen year olds, which we discovered the first night in a Belgian campsite bar. This certainly enlivened the games of table football and table tennis. Further juvenile amusement was derived from the labelling of the drink as 'Pils' and apparently pronounced as 'piss' - simple pleasures. There was also the learning curve of the strength of some of these lagers when one of the smaller boys had to be actually carried back to the tent after overindulgence. I suspect that consumptions were more closely monitored after this as the scout leader, (known to us as Bosun,) was the father of Bruce, one of my school friends and generally took his responsibilities as 'in loco parentis' very seriously. I don't recall any reoccurrences of over indulgence although the reaction the next day of the hungover one to a fried breakfast may have provided a deterrent to others.
Not all my hard earned money was spent on Pils as there were other temptations such as sheath knives and lighters in the shape of guns. Gifts were bought to take home and I recall a miniature cuckoo clock bought in Luxembourg and a table lamp in the shape of a sailing ship from Amsterdam. We were at that age immune to accusations of cliche or issues of poor

taste. Flag pennants were also popular to confirm that

we were now international travellers.
Highlights of the visit were boat trips on the
Amsterdam canals, viewing Brussels from the
Atonium, a futuristic a shiny building comprising a
number of huge connected chromium balls joined by
escalators. It stood over 300 feet high and was built
for the 1958 World fair and was the most eccentric
building I had ever seen. We were also in Coblenz for
a festival called the 'Rhine in Flames' which had a
procession of lit up barges sailing down the river
alongside the city camp-site and culminating in a
firework display which was more spectacular than
firework displays of the time at home.
I vaguely recall some amateurish attempts to chat up
local girls at a funfair but the fact we had to wear our
scout uniforms, including shorts when off site seemed
to contradict the cliche that 'all the girls love a man in
uniform' - maybe it doesn't apply to 15 year old scouts
and German schoolgirls.
My attempts at photography were limited to one
35mm slide film and I only see to have a small
number of that survived. This would seem strange

today when we all have the ability to record thousands of digital images with our phones. Also I seem to have recorded images that were novel for me rather than recording my fellow scouts which is a pity.

The weather was much warmer on the continent than at home that summer and the idyll was only marred by one event - England winning the World Cup. One tradition of travelling abroad was that Union Jack flag badges were sewn onto our scout uniforms and rucksacks. As well as prearranged football matches with Dutch and German scout troops, which I am pretty sure we lost most of, there were also ad hoc campsite kick-a-bouts where continental cousins were anxious to prove that the England Cup final victory, if not a home team fix, was a fluke and not to be repeated. In fact history seems to have borne out this early opinion but I do reflect that a better tactic would have been to establish with them at the outset that we were from Wales and at that time, before the Gareth Bale era, the nation was not a serious world soccer contender. (I have since learned that Wales had previously qualified for the World Cup in 1958 so my contention my be open to dispute.)
On the other hand it may have been the newly enjoyed supplies of Pils and chips with mayonnaise that was our undoing.

The next term back at school, after the summer holidays, studies were to begin in earnest for our GCE O level courses and I think my parents recommended

I concentrate on my school work perhaps worrying that my early rising for the paper round would sap my youthful energies. So I was to temporarily leave the newly entered world of work to concentrate on my academic education.

At school I didn't really think too much about a future career and for those us who stayed on after 16, which was the age it was possible to leave school at that time, the emphasis was to gain good A level grades and get into university. The school was a traditional red brick boys grammar school that clearly thought well of itself. Every autumn term the head would proudly list the names of pupils who had left the previous term and been accepted into Oxford and Cambridge, followed by a reasonably lengthy list of the ex-sixth formers entering other universities although they were not deemed as worthy of naming. I later discovered that a number of senior staff, as well as having distinguished themselves in wartime service, were also themselves graduates of Oxbridge. Given this, it may have been disrespectful for us to use the traditional humorous nicknames that had been attached to them e.g 'Monkey' and 'Dumbo' for prominent or hairy ears, 'Hairy' for a prematurely bald master, 'Buzzer' for another with a speech impediment that may have been vibrato caused by poorly fitting false teeth.

So it wasn't surprising that we were encouraged to set our horizons at what some may conclude an unrealistically high level. This had been set early when we we were to select our option subjects to take for our O levels.
We were told that certain universities and certainly Oxbridge colleges insisted on their prospective entrants having, in addition to the obligatory English and Maths, at least one foreign language and Latin as well as one science subject, even if they were prospective arts students. In the pre-Google days the

validity of these claims were impossible to check out, as a result of this I spent two years struggling with French and Physics before actually obtaining unspectacular but at least pass grades in both. I had chosen physics as chemistry seemed confusing and I was too squeamish for the dissection of animals in biology despite having been an enthusiastic fisherman. Latin was a dead end for me and I failed the O level after two years of conjugating and declining and translating the Iliad and Caesar's Gallic Wars. Although at the time I strongly resented having to study it, in later years I admit to finding it useful to understand the derivation and meanings of many English words so there is a lesson there that some experiences only have value some time later. Still I am not sure my rudimentary physics knowledge has ever proved useful to me!

At some point we were offered career advice as well as trying to select university subjects for study there was some superficial attempt to career counsel by an external careers advisor, I had already decided that I wanted to go on to university encouraged by tales from friend's elder brothers of the fine life they were living away from home. Along with other friends I had already been put off alternative of getting a job and starting a career straight away after a conversation, possibly at youth club with an old friend who already was an articled clerk at a firm of accountant's locally. He described the work as boring, the pay derisory and the hours long, to even include Saturday mornings!

I don't recall the advisor using any sophisticated techniques such as psychometric tests or questionnaires, it just seemed a bit of a rambling chat. The chemistry wasn't great, after I had mentioned the A-level subjects I was taking and my having expressed a preference to study economics at university he started to quiz me about what career this would lead to, which as I had no idea, I began to become defensive and suggested this was some way off. He then became to my mind somewhat aggressive which

11

did little to help the dialogue so I probably clammed up. He went on to explore career options should I become unsuccessful in getting to university. Anxious to bring the uncomfortable conversation to an end as soon as possible I rejected all the possibilities he offered. In frustration he finally proposed that being a Career Advisor was a good career! I had lost all respect for him and the process by this point and suggested we were wasting each other's time so I would now leave which I did. I was later taken to one side by my form master who expressed surprise that I had been so confrontational and thought it out of character having generally been seen as an amiable form member, having co-edited a form year newspaper and recently been made a prefect. When I told him of the conclusion that I could become a careers advisor he had trouble suppressing his laughter and we concluded that maybe I had a point in describing it as a waste of time. Happily I did get a university place and was thus able to delay a career selection for another few years. Again, I don't remember much direction being given over which universities to apply to. The school library was supplied with a stock of current university prospectuses, I don't recall any weekend trips to campuses away either by myself or any of my friends. When I arrived there many fellow students admitted this was their first visit and had applied 'blind' as such, some on the basis that one of their parents had studied there some decades before. Maybe a lot of life was more random at that time, certainly we didn't have the information overload of today.

Holiday Work

In future, until I finished university, the world of work was limited to holiday jobs. These included over the next few years: shop work, office work, farm work, building sites and steelworks. I like to think that I persevered in all of those environments and learnt valuable lessons for when I entered a full-time career. The only job I remember walking out of was when early one school holiday, I think in the sixth form, along with two school friends I answered an advert for a commission based job, selling door to door. I say 'selling door to door,' we didn't get any further than the door to the upstairs rented office which was the address we had been given when answering the small ad in the local paper.

It stated something like : 'Unemployed? Students? - Want to earn extra cash? Sales Opportunity, Free training given.'

Once we had taken our seats in an upstairs room in a terraced Victorian House on Walter Road, in town, (a road at that time full of solicitors, accountants and business premises of other professions,) we took in our surroundings. There were a dozen of us sitting on the assortment of hard chairs around the edge of the room, we appeared the youngest but all of us seemed under thirty years of age. The only other contents of the room were a couple of plain, tall cardboard boxes and a large faded carpet in the centre. A middle aged man dressed in a suit came into the room and welcomed us with a confident booming voice. He introduce himself and asked his first question -" Do any of you have experience of selling?" Although I had from an earlier holiday job I judged it prudent not to admit this at such an early point in proceedings. Another attendee was more anxious to demonstrate his experience by tentatively half raising an arm. For this he was subjected to a barrage of questions to which the suited man gave the answers without waiting for a reply.

"What's the most important skill for successful selling" - CONFIDENCE!
"How do you build confidence" - CLOSE SALES!
"Do you want to succeed in selling?" -OF COURSE YOU DO!
All delivered in a booming voice.
It's a long time ago so I am hazy about the details but the monologue went on for some time with no participation by the audience of prospective sales trainees.
At last, after some minutes of pretty unsubtle cod psychology, the pumped up Sales Guru, lugged one of the tall boxes onto the carpet and dramatically opened it up to reveal - an upright vacuum cleaner!! Cliche of cliches, we were prospective door-to- door, vacuum cleaner salespersons!
Out of nowhere, like a magician, he produced a bag of dust and sprinkled it liberally over the centre of the carpet. Then, possibly as part of the hands on training, the person nearest the power point on the wall was instructed to plug in. The carpet was then vigorously 'hoovered' by the non-hoover vacuum and we were told there would be a ten minute break for a tea break or for any smokers (it was the 1960's!) to go outside. The three of us went downstairs and outside - even though two of us didn't smoke.
"Are we going back in?" - fairly rapidly we all agreed we had seen enough and legged it. So we probably missed helpful hints on how to put your foot in a door, produce bags of dust from nowhere and other useful life skills but we had no regrets.

I mentioned that I had some previous sales experience. This was gained in a department store in the town where my Dad was the office manager and accountant. He heard that temporary staff were being taken on for their sales period and this coincided with one of my school holidays. I think I must have been 15 or 16 and in my O level year at school and eager to earn some money. I was to work in the men's knitwear

14

section and I guess it must have been the winter sales. The most memorable thing about the experience, the first I think of three spells working there, was that years later when watching the TV series of 'Are You Being Served?' Set in a similar store, I became convinced that the script writer must have worked in the very same shop as the characters were all there in the store. Having travelled more widely and witnessed similar shops, (mostly now gone,) I realise that the Swansea one was one of many. Later I was to see Bobbys in Folkestone and Worthing, Shinners in Sutton, Alders in Croydon, Hoopers in Tunbridge Wells and Hanningtons in Brighton.

There were common characters, shop uniforms, floor walkers in suits, matronly ladies in the children's departments, cashiers and caretakers.

The sales training was rudimentary and briefly provided to me by the permanent knitwear salesman Richard, a jovial thirty year old who consumed large pastries at his tea breaks as well as a generous lunch. He was supportive and explained that commission was paid on sales as well as the weekly pay packet. He kindly said that if a transaction got too complex for me I could always pass the customer over to him to complete the sale, (although I couldn't see this being necessary as my mental arithmetic was excellent and I wasn't planning on subsidising his pastry supply at the expense of my anticipated commission.) He passed on words of wisdom about sizing, warning me that families often came in with several sons of varying ages to be kitted out with new knitwear in the sales and it was often best to 'sell up' larger sizes to the children by suggesting that the child 'appeared small for their age.' Also that some of these families were from the farming community and were used to haggling from their times at markets and auctions. We weren't to ever consider a reduction but it was often useful to emphasise the reductions from the original prices which were shown on the label alongside the sale price. A swift mental calculation of the percentage

15

often helped secure a sale. His advice was put into practice quite early on when a ruddy faced farmer in a tweed suit leading three sons, the eldest not much smaller than me, arrived to be served.

"I want three good pullovers for each boy, heavy wool, long sleeved, hard wearing, no rubbish." He seemed to be in a hurry and suggested only the largest boy need to try them on and then additional ones could be supplied in different colours if available for the other two. He selected some heavy Jaeger jumpers which had a decent reduction from the original price but were only available in adult sizes. The larger boy took an adult medium which seemed a generous fitting but the father seemed satisfied and suggested smaller sizes for the other two sons, the smaller of which looked about nine and was under four foot tall. I found six more in adult small but was convinced that they would be much too big. I tentatively suggested they might like at least to try one on for size.

"No, no time - have to get back for milking," confirming Richard's assessment when they had come through the door.

"Wrap them up - and let me know the damage."

Even at the sale price it seemed quite a large purchase but the farmer peeled off a number of five pound notes from a thick roll of notes he produced from the inside pocket of his jacket. I wrote out the sales note and took it with the notes to the cashier, a young lady who sat inside a glass fronted cubicle which contained the despatch point for the air powered tube system which shot a small canister containing the money and the sales note up to the office on the top floor where I guess sales and stock ledger entries were made. In short order the system shot back the receipt and any change due for the sale.

The wait for the change and receipt to be returned from the cash desk seemed to add to my unease and I was eager to say "you could bring them back if they don't fit." Despite being instructed that sales goods would not normally be exchanged.

16

I was relieved when I had wrapped up their purchases and they left the store.

Richard said "Well done, a good sale." But the commission, calculated at some 2p in the pound didn't seem to compensate for my unease in expecting the farmer to return leading a small boy with a jumper down to his knees and demanding to see the conman who had sold it to them. It was at least a week before I stopped nervously glancing at new groups of children and their parents coming into the shop and looking out for an angry red faced farmer in a tweed suit.

I am not sure what my learning experience was from this - maybe that the retail world is a risky place full of the tricks of the trade. I guess that I learned that quickly as at some other time, maybe my next school holiday, I was employed in the school uniform department. Not sure why, as I would have preferred to work in knitwear with Richard who was easy going and the manager of the school uniforms had a slight Mrs Slocombe manner about her, (without the double entendre feline references!)

The couple of other young assistants seem slightly in dread of her so I was warned to tread carefully. The first day she said somewhat dismissively that she supposed I would be of some use as I was closer in age to the likely customers which seemed to be an early attempt to belittle me. Rather than reply with some derogatory reference to the decades since her own schooldays I kept my counsel. The next exchange was more up my street.

"What do you say if we only have a blazer in a too large size for the child - do you know?"

Thanks to my earlier experience in knitwear I was able to reply -

'Well you ask their age and then say that they seem very small and are probably due a growing spurt soon.'

I am not sure I ever resorted to that tactic as the commission rate was clearly not going to ever change my life.

This was the right answer and I seemed to have got on her good side, at least temporarily. I think I was only working in that department there for a couple of weeks and was pleased that a later holiday saw me back in knitwear again.

The lesson learned was that there are recognised practices in working environments and not all of them are developed with the best of intentions and maybe you don't always need to follow the herd.

The other work experience that came from this shop was during the next sales period when instead of selling in the shop I was given the task of mailing out publicity leaflets to their registered customer list. This was the 1960's and pre-desk top publishing and widespread use of computerised mailing lists. The whole exercise was 'hand written' from large bound ledgers of their account holders and registered customers which ran to several thousands. A task so large I was allowed to enrol a couple of my school friends, so armed with boxes of pens, envelopes and leaflets we were set up in a separate building upstairs in Wind Street, several doors down from the actual shop. I don't really remember the details whether it was a day rate or a fixed price but I do remember we became more proficient at it and set up a sort of production line, folding the leaflets, addressing the envelopes etc rotating the tasks every hour or so for variety. I suspect there was an anticipated daily volume which we found to be easy to meet and slightly exceed but not by so much that it would reduce our earnings. So over the couple of weeks the task took we would take it in turns to absent ourselves and go out for a coffee or to the record booths in Boots or the Co-op.

It was an early lesson in the importance of managing a task even when it has been delegated as I don't remember anyone coming to check our progress as long as we returned several completed boxes of addressed and filled envelopes at the end of each day.

The other unusual experience I remember which was either a tribute to my flexibility (or more likely how expendable I was to the sales team) and it was to occur one morning during the winter sales. There were forecasts of snow and it was decided the weekly stock replenishment of the satellite shops further into West Wales would still need to be done. I was initially pleased with the suggestion that I should accompany the van driver on his run that day to restock the branches. I felt a certain disquiet when one of the store staff offered us both some pairs of gloves and woolly hats from the stockroom and this sense grew significantly when two large shovels and some old sacking was casually tossed in the back of the van. It occurred to me, as I said goodbye to Richard, that his greater bulk might have been of more use both in strength of pushing a van stuck in snow and also in providing greater ballast for grip on icy roads. Perhaps there wasn't room in the full van for his break time snacks and lunch or more likely he didn't want to risk not getting home for his dinner.

From memory the department store had branches in Llanelli, Carmarthen and in the far west, Haverfordwest. All went well to Llanelli and we unloaded the stock and collected some returns and clothes for alterations. At Carmarthen we had a quick cafe lunch after leaving the shop and headed off west to Haverfordwest, noticing the sky was ominously darker and the air had a distinct chill outside the warmth of the van.

The driver was good company, familiar with the roads as he had driven the route many times and wasn't worried about the weather which was reassuring. After all this time I am afraid I can't remember his name so we'll call him Dave for narrative purposes. Midway between Carmarthen and Haverfordwest the snow started, light at first but quickly getting heavier. Dave became much quieter and I think we both started to contemplate a night stranded in the van, possibly in a snowdrift!

After some minutes the snow eased off and Dave, (as we now know him,) cheerfully announced we would reach Haverfordwest in about half an hour, adding if all goes well which wasn't reassuring. He was right and the roads seemed to still be clear but we didn't bother hanging about for the offered cup of tea or coffee from the shop manager once we had unloaded the van. Looking at the darkening sky it was agreed that we'd better set off for the return journey without delay. All went well until we got just east of Carmarthen when the snow fall came down with a vengeance and the van started to lose grip on hills eventually sliding off onto the verge and refusing to move out of a few inches of snow. It looked like there had been falls earlier in the day here and the new snow just served to compound difficulties. By use of the sacking under the wheels we were eventually back onto the road although Dave didn't help by saying the van would handle better if more heavily loaded. It made me wonder whether he was wishing for a helper of more generous proportions but resisted suggesting this to him. After a few more sticky patches the road nearer the coast became much clearer and the late afternoon sky brightened up before sunset. Driving to the back of the store the staff opening the double doors at the loading bay commented cheerfully that we were lucky it hadn't snowed. I showed them the wet bottoms of my trouser legs and silently handed them my soaking wet gloves and woolly hat. So ended my first experience of riding shotgun on a Welsh polar expedition.

Another job I had as a youngster had a more direct relationship of effort to reward and I think it was my only experience of 'piecework.' This was on a farm in Gower and it started with runner bean picking as a 6th former and in pre-decimal days the rate was two old shillings for a full crate. A number of us went along,

20

working between the tall rows of climbing beans and as a summer job, even in Wales, it could get warm between the rows of beans. We started early to avoid the heat of the day and picked from 8 through until between 1 or 2 in the early afternoon when as 17 and 18 year olds we would adjourn, thirsty, to the nearest village pub for well earned beers and ploughman's lunches of bread, pickles and cheese. I believe the pub has now been gentrified and won accolades as one of the best 'gastro pubs' in Wales. I doubt if ploughman's lunches still feature.

Feeling we were entitled as agricultural workers, albeit temporary ones, to indulge in the full cliche. If we had earned enough to support our evening out and a contribution to the petrol for whichever's friends mothers car we had hijacked we would spend the afternoon on the beach.

Sometimes we were energetic enough to return to the farm for a couple more hours but usually the morning's efforts were enough for our needs. I remember them as idyllic days and it must have been an unusual dry Welsh summer as I don't recall us being rained off. As we had established ourselves with the farmer and his wife we were sometimes redeployed on other duties including picking broad beans. This wasn't so popular as the plants were prickly and scratched our arms and legs and although it was still piece work it was more back breaking and I think, less rewarding, financially. Another time we were entrusted with a tractor and a tow behind potato harvester so we would take it in turns to drive it as a relief from sorting potatoes, from the earth and stones, on the conveyor belt it towed. I think that was a flat day rate and not so lucrative for a longer day, also both those tasks didn't benefit from the shade provided by the climbing beans and more than one of us were sunburnt.

I was grateful for winter Xmas job being indoors. Several months previously a number of us had registered for part-time Xmas post jobs with the Post Office, This was the end of my first terms at university and I remember it as a harsh winter with snow in December before Xmas. I was pleased to be told that I was allocated to the sorting office and not out on the delivery rounds and was even more grateful when I met friends coming back in at the end of their rounds, tired and cold. My duties seemed to be taking sacks of collected mail and doing a pre-sort into areas before putting them onto trolleys and delivering them to the sorters who would do a final sort into road and street order in pigeon holes. It was all very friendly and it didn't seem like hard work and the money was a useful addition to the next term's grant. It was interesting to compare experiences with other students there from different universities, I recall that there was some meeting up outside the office in the pubs and disco's in Gower and Mumbles hotels. All in all it made up for missing the new friends and social life away at university. I don't remember any useful learning from the workings of the then GPO other than it seemed pretty labour intensive to get a piece of paper from one place to another. I guess if I had been Steve Jobs I would have invented email on the spot but I did learn that work was an easy place to meet new people.

The lessons learnt from all the various jobs in different environments were that people use different skills in their occupations and that you should not see any job as inferior to another. I was often in awe of fellow shop staff when dealing with awkward and snooty customers and learnt from the patience shown when I would have felt like suggestion they take their business and lack of manners elsewhere. The lessons learnt were valuable later in my own career when dealing with difficult customers and colleagues. I also realised that all employment carries a certain degree of problem solving and maybe it's this that makes work interesting. It also allows an individual a certain freedom as how they do their job and this is important because it makes us human and to try and reduce an individual to a repetitive machine is a serious mistake.

Real Money

At the end of my first year at university I returned home with a number of things:-
Firstly, a full beard and shoulder length hair, (it was 1970.)

Secondly, and better news to my parents, I had heard that the results in the end of first year exams were good enough for me to enter the second year. At that time it was alleged that my faculty 'sent down' up to 20 % of the first year social study students with the lowest marks in their exams at the end of the third term. This was something we lived in dread of and encouraged a higher work rate in the third term among those if us wanting to perpetuate this idyllic lifestyle.

Lastly, as a result of the idyllic lifestyle I had spent all of my grant, as well as savings and some of the bank's money so I had acquired an overdraft as had most of my university friends who had enjoyed the idyllic lifestyle with me. Much of the expenditure had been on records and hangovers and not wanting to sell my precious records and the market for second hand hangovers yet to be monetised I needed a job!
In those days although it was called the Employment exchange rather than being rebranded the snappier titled 'Job Centre,' rather than go in for counselling and skill analysis and other New Age stuff it did indeed carry details of jobs on offer.
The next day after the visit I found myself in a cafe being 'interviewed,' in a broad Brummie accent by a construction contractor for some kind of temporary building job at a large building site project in Swansea. At that time it was vaguely described as the Driving

License Offices, later known as the DVLC, (now the DVLA.) It was being built on a greenfield site on the outskirts of Swansea and was part of the initiative programme of that time to export jobs in government departments out of London to the provinces. Similar initiatives included the Royal Mint relocating to Llantrisant, allowing the dubious joke of labelling it 'the Hole with the Mint,' as a corruption of the current advert for Polo Mints.

I started to research this movement but the density and verbosity of the papers and journals describing this started to give me a headache and I thought that if I can't be bothered to wade through them then you probably aren't that interested either. If you are there's a lot of material to be read so good luck with that. I know that a friend relocated from Central London to Swindon and my reluctant dealings with the Inland Revenue were conducted from Newcastle.

But returning to Swansea it appears that Sal, (I never found out what it was abbreviated from and he seemed a bit too masculine to have been christened Sally,) had secured the contract to install the air conditioning plant for the computer hall that was the central brain of the Licensing Centre and I was to be a key member of his team in achieving it. The interview was cursory and seemed to consist of whether I had experience of physical work, I think the reference to farm work impressed him.

'Where did I live?' And could I be available at 7.30 a.m? I bluffed an enthusiastic answer to this as it appeared he could collect me in Sketty on his way to the site.

With any luck I may be able to doze in the car unless I was trying to translate a broad Brummie morning conversation. At university I had encountered plenty of regional accents and was getting more attuned to them. There was one blunder when I asked one student from Northumberland which part of Ireland they came from.

24

The best thing was that the hourly rate seemed generous so my look of pleasure was met with a blunt comment of 'It'll be hard work - I am working to deadlines and I can't be doing with any time wasters.' Chastened, I shook hands with him and it was agreed he would pick me up at the end of my road at 7.30 and with a 'be there on time - I won't wait.'

I was at the agreed meeting place the next morning five minutes before time after setting an alarm clock and using the bathroom even before my Dad. Sal seemed pleased I was on time and chatted happily en route which put paid to my planned nap. He also explained there would be another worker there who had also been recruited from the Job Centre. Arriving at the building site where our part was a set of concrete foundations that already had some sort of low metal framework of steel girders about a foot off the ground. Shortly after we arrived a slight blonde haired teenager turned up right on time and was introduced as Chris. I thought I recognised him and it transpired he was a year below me at school and had just completed his 'A' levels.

Sal outlined briefly what was to happen. We were to construct from prefabricated metal a kind of cooling tower as part of the air-conditioning plant for the site's computer room. Some of the parts would be lifted on site by crane and we would bolt them together. Once built the towers would contain filters to allow the water to drop down through it and would be cooled by large fans fitted into the sides of the plant. The work would need to be carried out with care and the weight and size of the parts brought in by crane made it dangerous and we would need to closely follow Sal's instructions. We were given sturdy gloves and advised to wear boots and I was relieved that my hiking boots that I had decided to wear met with approval.

The first couple of days went ok as we were working at ground level but Chris had already irritated Sal by turning up in plimsoles on day one and turning up late on the third day. At the end of the week the crane was

25

deployed to bring in some large steel panels that we were to manhandle into place and the danger was apparent as Sal barked out instructions to hold it or move it one way or another. As it was held in place, one of us pushed a metal rod into one of the holes lined up on the edge of the plate and the girder. For some reason, (all trades have their jargon!) Sal would call to "Podger" which meant to push the rod into the lined up holes and sometimes he would call "Hammer" and we would encourage the holes to align by hammered persuasion.

The work seemed to have an element of danger but I could see Sal was experienced and gave clear and timely instructions. On that day Chris seemed hesitant and didn't always seem to hear the instructions, much to our employer's frustration. God knows what the modern day 'Risk assessment culture,' would have made of this heavy engineering task assisted by two teenagers.

On Monday when I was picked up Sal said "I don't think Chris will turn up today and if he does I think I'll have to tell him he's not up to it." Sure enough, he was right and by 9.30 there was no sign of him.

"Let's go for breakfast - I have something to ask you." We went to a local cafe for a welcome fry up and I hoped Sal was going to ask me if I knew of someone to replace Chris and was mentally listing friends I knew who were back from university and both free for work and who wouldn't mind being shouted at and risking being crushed by metalwork, for money. Sal ordered our breakfasts and gently teased me when I ordered coffee instead of tea which I much preferred, generating a comment if " Huh - Students."

Once we were sitting down his proposal surprised me. "You are doing ok, you understand what's needed and just do it, that's good, we can work together well. How about I pay you fifty percent more, half of what I had to pay Chris and we complete the job together. That way we both benefit and I think we can make good progress."

26

It only took seconds to agree - it would be the fastest and largest, by percentage, pay rise I would get in my entire working life!

As the construction continued over the coming weeks I got fitter, richer and overcame a fear of heights, as long as I had something solid to hang onto. The construction went well and I even took a long weekend off at the end of June to go to the Bath Festival. This wasn't a weekend of chamber and orchestral music but one of the UK's first large scale rock festivals that had followed Woodstock in the US, held outside New York the previous summer. Music was an important part of our lives in the 1960's and 70's and having recently seen the film of Woodstock, the opportunity of seeing some of the same bands live was too good an opportunity to miss.

Researching the line ups I came up with some overlaps between Woodstock, the Bath Festival and the Isle of Wight 1970 festival later the same summer. The artists from Woodstock also at Bath were mostly American and included:-

Country Joe, John Sebastian, Canned Heat, Jefferson Airplane and Johnny Winter. There were also the UK band who had also been there, The Keef Hartley band. When I later went to the Isle of Wight festival the artists appearing there as well as at Woodstock included John Sebastian, Ten Years After, The Who, Richie Havens and Jimi Hendrix, (sadly in his final live performance.)

At Bath there were other bands not at Woodstock who were great to see including, Pink Floyd, Led Zeppelin, Steppenwolf, Frank Zappa, the Byrds, John Mayall and Dr John.

I remember a mostly acoustic set from Donovan who appeared to have been pushed on stage after the rain had maybe caused problems for the set up and won over the crowd with a long set.

All this was in the future as I finished work early at the building site that Friday afternoon and stood at the outskirts of Swansea with a small rucksack and a sleeping bag, with my thumb out. I was lucky as the first car that stopped for me was a Morris Minor en route to the festival itself and full of hairy blokes from Pembrokeshire and a certain amount of heady, pungent fumes. It was a good natured trip and offers of payment towards petrol were waved away. Arriving in the evening the roads were very congested and thanking my lift-givers I left the traffic jam to walk to the site along with a stream of other people, the greatest number of long haired and bearded people I had seen, outside the footage from Woodstock. I had hoped to meet up with old school friends travelling from Swansea but the long walk to the site and hunger after a hard day at the building site meant food was a priority. If I had been prepared, and I should have been after my years in the Scouts, I should have been carrying at least some snacks but no, I was 19 and carefree, at least for the weekend, so I trusted to chance.

I wasn't really prepared for the scene that met me later that evening as I came to the gates to the site and could see into the fields beyond. Tens of thousands of people many sitting in huddled groups, interspersed with small tents and the occasional large marquee stretched down the hillside towards an large empty lit stage with speaker stacks at the side. I realised that it must have been the largest crowd that I had ever been part of. Music was playing, not loudly, and it was being soaked up by the crowd and there was no one playing on the stage. How would I ever find my friends ?

Once in through the gates, surrendering my ticket bought in a record store in Swansea, I set out to find some food. It was not too difficult although the sky had darkened and it looked like rain. People were wending their way towards me carrying open bags of chips, filled buns and cans of drink. Tracing the direction they had come from I joined a long queue in front of one of the food stalls in a tent. Everyone was very polite and friendly and I soon got into conversation with the people next to me who had no bags and said they had hitched from Brighton and met up earlier with some friends who were looking after their bags and bedding. Asking how they had managed to meet,(remember we were an unconnected generation, phones were tied to the wall then!) They recommended going to the Release tent, next to the first aid tent and that would have a large Red Cross on it.They explained that there were large boards there and you could pin a message there to arrange a future meet up or give directions to a friend's tent.

I thought this was a task for the next day and once I had bought a drink and some hot food I went with my 'new friends' back to a nearby large marquee in the corner of which, along with a few of their mates, they had set up camp. This turned out to be a good plan as it rained in the night and many other who hadn't had shelter had to make the best of it under plastic sheets or coats. The morning found them drying these out in the welcome sunshine. I had slept like a log despite being surrounded by many other sleeping strangers. I guess a necessary toilet call was made but as these are often the stuff of legend at festivals, and not an attractive legend, thankfully like many aspects of the weekend I have no memory of this. I must have managed to find a drink and some breakfast doubtless involving lengthy queueing and then searched for the notice boards I had been told about.

Again, the actual details are lost to me but I think by placing SWANSEA Friends in capital letters in red felt tip and a suggested time back at the board I was able to meet the group of half a dozen Swansea friends who had travelled together and then join them on their allotted patch of grass. We were later joined by Guy, my university friend whom I must have made contact with in the same way and the weekend was set to begin in earnest. Live music had started on stage and my group of friends had come better prepared than me, with food and drinks and large groundsheets which doubled as an ad hoc shelter during showers. The next two days are a little blurry due to uncomfortable sleep and intoxicants including chemically enhanced yogurts! The music and company was great - I particularly enjoyed Santana, Led Zeppelin who gave what is reckoned to be one of their best performances, Pink Floyd, (in the early hours of Sunday morning,) and It's a Beautiful Day who impressed me enough to buy their album later. It really felt like we were part of the 60's revolution surrounded by tens of thousands of like minded denim clad long hairs. The crowd was estimated to be over 200,000 which I knew to be the approximate population of my home town but everyone in Swansea hasn't gathered in the same field for a weekend or at least if they had I wasn't invited. The following Tuesday back at work and still recovering Sal asked if it was any good and whether many had turned up? As the saying goes -"You had to have been there!"

The construction was completed in the next six or seven weeks with the last week spent fixing together thousand of plastic trays like large egg trays that would go inside the tank to slow the passage of water down through it, allowing the large cooling fans more time to do their work. I realised after this I would now longer be needed on site so started to plan more holiday activities.

Having enjoyed the festival experience later that summer a group of us travelled to Radnorshire for the Knighton free festival driving on a few days afterwards to the second Isle of Wight festival notable for the last live performances by the Doors with Jim Morrison and Jimi Hendrix. I took the precaution of travelling with friends this time to avoid the stresses of 'meet me by the First Aid tent at 12 o'clock' messages.

The Isle of Wight festival was again massive and probably attended by even more than at Bath. This didn't stop us reuniting with our friend Vernon who woke us up in our tent by tripping over our guy rope and swearing loudly in a voice we instantly recognised. As we said to him and his sister with him - 'what were the odds of that.'

At the end of the festival the plan was to drive to a party in Hull, these were freewheeling times though not for my friend Geoff's mother's mini that burned it's clutch out near Bristol with the strain of carrying five of us. Undaunted two pairs of us went on to hitch the rest of the way unkindly abandoning him to sort it out promising to meet in Hull, at least that's what I thought he said.

I don't remember if I returned to work again before the start of term. I had probably earned enough money by then for my needs as well as invaluable lessons on the workings of cooling plants for computer systems, should I ever need to build another one, (I never have!)

More worryingly for several years if I heard that anyone had delays in getting their car tax or driving licence from Swansea I wasn't entirely sure the problem wasn't an overheated computer centre.

This lengthy digression may seem separate from the world of work but there are a few linked thoughts. Work is not an end in itself but it allows you to gain other experiences both at work but also through using down time to pursue other interests many of which require the money earned through work.

The other experience I took from going to the festival was a reinforcement of a feeling, already present, that I was part of a different generation and our world and the world of our work would differ from our parent's generation and previous ones.

More of this later.

The next holiday job was in a steelworks, I did live in Wales after all but had no ambition to go down a mine despite making the mistake of joining the university caving club. After only two rather claustrophobic caving trips I took a back seat in the club limiting my involvement to social events and crewing for the

Caving club in the annual university Rag week raft race. I didn't actually produce any steel and from what I could see the plant fabricated pipes etc from steel plates. The factory floor was noisy and potentially dangerous with overhead gantry cranes lifting and conveying huge sheets of steel onto impressive machines for rolling and bending. I wasn't involved in any of this and was assigned to a maintenance gang as a labourer. The gang called me Prof on account of my four terms at university and for the first couple of days had some fun with me. Whilst not actually sending me to the stores to collect sky hooks or a bucket of compressed air they did indulge in me having to mix mortar by hand at one end of the works before 'deciding' it was to be used several hundred yards away and needed taking there, by me, in a wheel barrow with a wobbly wheel.

Particularly risky with welding sparks, fork-lifts whizzing about and the sheets of steel coming through the air dangling from the cranes. I persevered with this, the pay was good, (and I had another overdraft to clear as well as my first old car to run) and it was making me fit. I thought they would tire of this soon and after I had joined them for fry up breakfasts and beers at lunch time on payday the fun stopped. I was declared an honorary one of the gang and welcomed back again for a couple more weeks the following holiday with questions like -

'what did you learn this time Prof ?'

I wondered whether to impart my newly acquired knowledge of macroeconomics or the New Deal but thought better of it. I had learnt that it was necessary to become one of the tribe to more easily survive but also that individuality and differences were tolerated as long as some of the tribal norms were adhered to. As in this case it included teamwork, such as ensuring the bricklayers, who regarded as the elite of the maintenance gang, were kept supplied with sufficient mortar at the right time made to the right consistency. Adopting the social mores such as swearing

32

sufficiently, eating fried foods and buying your round of beer also helped, none of which I found difficult. Had I been a teetotal, puritanical vegan it might have been more difficult but these were in short supply in South Wales in the early 1970's or at least they were in the steelworks and universities.

I took my tea breaks with another member of maintenance, Terry who was the one nearest my age but clearly from a different fashion tribe, with drain pipes and a short haired Elvis hair style, he was more of a rocker. Tall and rangy, he carried himself in confident way and moved the heavy stuff around effortlessly. One Friday he invited me to go to a weekend dance in a venue in Llanelli with him and his mates. "Come along Prof, you'll enjoy it - have you got some decent threads ?"

'Er-what?'

"A smart suit, shirt and tie."

My 1970's look was much more Woodstock and I think my smart jacket was a corduroy sports coat from sixth form.

'I am going to a friend's party in Mumbles this weekend - but thanks, maybe another time,' I said making my excuses.

I never did take up the offer but it was nice to be asked and could have been interesting.

One of the older brickies in the team must have overheard - he quietly said to me -

"Don't worry - if you go, Terry will take care of you, he's the king of the Teds in Llanelli   And no-one messes with him or his mates. I had my entree into Carmarthenshire gangland, as long as I had a decent suit.

I have limited my reminiscences here to jobs I had while at school and university rather than talking about the actual academic work there. Those days are probably the material for a whole new set of writings but there are some thoughts from those days that I took as lessons for my later career and life in general.

Lesson one remain curious. I have always retained an interest in others, what they are doing and what their interests are. I have found by doing this it takes you to unexpected places and I would rarely dismiss anyone's academic subject, career choice or hobby out of hand. I admit there are dangers here and you can get dragged into areas that you wonder how you got in this deep and where is the escape route. In this I would include my membership of Aberystwyth University Caving Society when I suspected all along that I had latent claustrophobia tendencies. A spell of owning a scooter when all along I knew that four is the minimum safe number of wheels for a vehicle, (in fact five to include the steering wheel and exclude any hare brained ideas about self-driving cars!) At university there were opportunities to learn more about the subjects your friends and flat mates were studying and through this I attended early music recitals, obscure foreign films, collected rock samples and hermit crabs and was introduced to obscure mathematical theories and computer programs.

I carried this interest over in adult life both in work and social situations and found that there is nothing that people like more than talking about something that they are passionate about. You never know when snippets of information gathered may be useful to you.

Lesson two, perfection and completeness is the road to madness.

The well worn cliche, 'life is full of compromises,' is very true in the workplace.

Given unlimited resources including time anyone can probably achieve almost anything but life isn't like that. There are always constraints on timescales, resources, finances, right skills and authorities. Given these the perfect solution is rarely achieved but a good solution delivered in time is often the best answer. I often used to say to people working with me on a project that we shouldn't work to supply a strong stainless steel component as a new or replacement addition to the organisation as we were working with an imperfect organisation made of soft wood held together by string and a new indestructible stainless steel component would shake the rest of the pieces apart and destroy them.

I hope you see the analogy.

Lesson three, concentrate on the objective not the methodology. With any task from a small one to the delivery of a large project I have found that people work best when allowed to use their own methods and the important thing is to emphasise the end objective not the means to get there.

Embrace change - it's going to happen anyway!

Looking for a Full Time Career

At last I started my full-time career and to do so I arrive one Sunday afternoon early in November outside the railway station in Folkestone, Kent. Carrying a suitcase containing a new suit and a smart pair of shoes, with the overflow in a rucksack on my back I checked into the first small hotel I found in walking distance of the station.

It was dark within an hour so it was later in the week that I could explore the town and catch sight of the English Channel and the French coast in the distance. The opportunity for full time employment had not been straight-forward. I hadn't thought I would stay in my home town of Swansea despite only having travelled away some two hours to university in Aberystwyth. South Wales was going through one of the periodic times of economic decline and graduate work opportunities were limited with many of them at the new Driving Licence Centre where I had inside knowledge that a system failure due to air conditioning problems in the computer centre could force its closure at any time. The alternatives to work had been dismissed quickly. Several fellow graduates were staying on in Aberystwyth, either to take a one year teaching certificate or a couple to complete Master's degrees. I really didn't fancy teaching despite having previously owned both a tweed and a corduroy jacket; items I knew to at least meet the sartorial entrance requirements. A masters degree exceeded my interest in both Economics and International Politics, the subjects that comprised my joint honours degree. It was definitely time for me to leave academia and enter the world of full time work.

The quest for this began during the previous spring when something occurred at university called the 'milk round.' I don't know if this still goes on but the events were some kind of job fair where companies and organisations travelled around to universities handing out leaflets about how wonderful it would be to work

36

for them and arrange on the spot preliminary interviews to be possibly followed up later at their place of work should you clear the first hurdle. This reading of brochures and time spent in interviews certainly cut into the busy schedule of socialising interrupted by a little light studying as well as lectures and seminars. The studying at this point in the third year hadn't yet reached the fever pitch it would shortly do at the start of the third term when the Finals examinations loomed.

I am not sure how I selected the companies to speak to and I don't think much science was applied to the process. I also don't remember any individual career advice being offered although the memory of that from school hadn't sufficiently diminished for me to have viewed it with suspicion had it been!

My memory is not comprehensive on this so there may have been others but I do know that I attended interviews for graduate traineeships with the Post Office, several large banks and insurance companies and for some reason the National Bus company. I also think there was an oil company but not sure which one. The bank interviews were a disaster with me looking like a member of a Californian rock band, or at least one of their road crew and across the table from me a couple of stereotypical short-haired bankers in pinstriped, three piece suits. One of which even said 'how do you expect us to take you seriously while you look like that?' which strangely was what I was also thinking about them and may even have said so. I am not sure what they were expecting on a campus in the early 1970's but after a similar experience with another bank I skipped the other appointments and gave up on a potential career in finance. Later in my career I was always amused to meet people in banking in a business context and tell them their industry was denied the opportunity of my talent through a cultural mismatch.

The Post Office and the National Bus company interviews went better with invites to later follow up interviews; the first was in the bus company's Swansea depot but then both followed up by London interviews. The Post Office included some aptitude exam/test which it seemed I didn't match up to their requirements, (despite having collected stamps as a child and played at post offices with a set which was popular at the time.)

I mention some traumatic bus related childhood incidents in my book 'A 1950's Boy.'

Wisely, I avoided mentioning this in London at the interview but I had taken the precaution of travelling to the London interview from Swansea on one of the so called express coaches which seemed anything but. Not only was the journey interminable but there was a lot of lengthy hanging about in several bus depots en route. Still 'bus lagged' from the journey I may have been a bit too blunt for them about this in the interview and I think I learnt that in corporate life sometimes the truth needs some sugar coating to be made palatable. I didn't know that then, so a career in transport, even one in the slow lane was not to be.

After the finals I had enjoyed the last few weeks of freedom being a student and now one without any studying and was able to spend time with friends from university and home. I certainly enjoyed my time at university in Aberystwyth. It's a picturesque seaside town with the only drawbacks being its exposure to storms from the Irish Sea, more worrying if you are a property or business owner worried about damage to your premises than it was to a student renting a flat. The other potential drawback is the distance from anywhere else and the limited transport links to get there but this means that the town has to rely on itself for culture and entertainment. Returning in recent years I found that shopping, eating and cultural facilities were much improved which isn't surprising given the passage of time.

I had spent the summer after university back in Swansea working as a labourer on a large car showroom restoration. It was being project managed by someone my father knew and I guess it was a case of someone knowing someone. I cannot see the building in the town centre now and I think a cinema and hotel have been built on the site. The building was being gutted by a large team of subcontractors and my joining them as a long haired student caused a similar amount if good natured teasing that I had experienced in the steelworks. I had learnt that earlier that it is important to fit in and my years of 'training' at university had equipped me well to cope with the large amounts of lunchtime beer on payday and the generous greasy breakfast fry ups and bacon rolls that at the time fuelled workers on building sites. I also realised it was best not to read the vacancy supplements of any of the broadsheets during tea or lunch breaks. Despite this my new colleagues were interested in my future career prospects and some of those with older children were interested in sensible discussions about the university experience. It was humbling for me to realise how relatively rare it was to obtain a university degree and a number of them welcomed the chance to speak to a recent graduate, perhaps for them the first time they had been able to do so outside formal settings such as parents evenings at school. I realised that these hard working people had the same ambitions for their families that had been held by my own parents and I hope I that my information about the opportunity that university gave me helped them with those ambitions.

The work was hard and required me on site at 8 a.m. and that summer I had moved into a student flat in Swansea with some old school friends and we continued some of the student lifestyles with late nights and partying. I think the bracing early morning walk to work in town from the flat in Brynmill helped to clear my head.

During my last term at Aberystwyth my parents had moved from Wales to Hertfordshire and at the end of the summer I moved there temporarily while I applied for a permanent job. While there I worked in the offices of a large building supplies company as a temp doing boring tasks to do with stock taking and sales volumes I think it was transferring paper records to computer input forms and I do remember it was mind numbing enough to almost put me off a career in administration. I was also hearing from friends staying in education and research which started to sound attractive. There were interviews with two local councils in the Home Counties and a couple of applications for graduate trainee positions. Fortunately, a successful interview with one of the councils for an uninspiring position as a committee secretary coincided with an interview invitation from an electricity board and I had a few days grace before my decision was needed.

Electricity

I am not sure where I saw the advert for Seeboard; I think it's likely to have been in the Recruitment section of the Sunday Times. The company, which I had never heard of before, was a regional electricity board for the South East based in Kent, Surrey and Sussex with their head office in Hove which meant Brighton to me. I am no longer clear on the timescale but believe it must have been September. At the time I was back staying with my parents at their home in Watford that they had recently moved to because of my Dad's work. In the days before the internet I had probably gone to the local reference library to attempt to gain some rudimentary knowledge about the organisation and I don't remember this being very fruitful. Despite my A level geography I recall I caught the train to Brighton station, not Hove which is several miles further west. This wasn't really a problem as I was travelling lightly with a small bag containing my suit and a clean shirt. I walked from the station through the shops eventually dropping down to the coast road and seafront promenade. I was looking for the address of the head office, described grandly as No. 1 Grand Avenue. After passing a couple of magnificent squares surrounded by tall pale regency terraces I finally found the offices and noting their position looked for a nearby B and B to book into for the night. I think it was a Sunday as the shops had been closed as they were in those days before Sunday trading but the seafront had been busy as it was a seaside resort on an early autumn weekend. I booked into the first bed and breakfast I found and after hanging up my clothes for the next day set out for a look around in the early evening. I was very impressed with what I saw and realised that I was looking forward to working in this grand sea front office which was presumptuous of me before I had even attended the interview. Returning to the B and B I had a quiet hour or two before thinking I would find somewhere to eat. Without local knowledge

41

and having a pretty strong constitution I chose a curry house figuring that a couple of accompanying beers would help settle any pre-interview nerves and help ensure a decent nights sleep. I needn't have worried as the travelling and walking around meant I slept like a log until I was awoken by my travel alarm clock.

Once I realise where I was and what lay ahead that day I ate a hearty breakfast followed by a walk along the seafront to fully wake me up. The interview itself that morning seems a long time ago and details are sketchy but I recall that I was welcomed in the reception of this large Victorian building by someone from the personnel department who announced I would be reimbursed for my travel and accommodation as long as I had receipts. Fortunately I had receipts even though I wasn't expecting this generosity although travel expenses had been paid to me before at interviews. Maybe I could have stayed in a grander hotel had I known. I was also given a slim brochure about the company which I eagerly scanned before being shown into a large conference style room where there were some other candidates, all smartly dressed in their best suits and most of them scanning their copies of the brochure. Reimbursed with unexpected funds and impressed with the seafront location of the office I was determined to give the interview my best shot so I was disappointed to hear during the introduction, given by a smiling man who described himself as Seeboard's head of training, that today was one of a number of graduate recruitment days that were being held. He also didn't elaborate on the number of positions that they were looking to fill and looking at other nervous expressions in the room I could see that others were of the same mind. The other reassurance was although we were all smartly dressed in business wear, predominantly young men in suits with a couple of women candidates, there were others with beards and hair long enough to give an army recruiting sergeant raised blood pressure or worse. After the experience with the banks I had now trimmed my hair and beard to more moderate length whilst still, I hoped complying with current fashion. There was some kind of group discussion, I believe but I can't remember any details. I guess we were being observed for signs of wisdom or insanity. There was a break for coffee when there was a chance for the gladiators, I mean fellow candidates, to chat. People had come from far and wide and from different universities having followed a range of courses. It had been explained to us in the introductory talk that the previous recruitment of graduate trainees had been exclusively engineering graduates and the organisation wanted to develop it's non engineering functions through fast tracking some graduates from other disciplines through a structured two year course before placing them in permanent positions. This all sounded very encouraging and the advertised starting salary was already some fifty percent higher than two recent jobs I had attended interviews for. Refreshed we returned to the conference room where we were handed a short written questionnaire to complete which, if my memory serves me correctly was an opportunity to expand on our CV's we had submitted and asked the usual questions about our strengths and what we thought we wanted out of a career and what we thought we brought to it. I had read and been told that this sort of thing required a careful balance between confidence and humility and phrases like 'wiling to learn', 'flexibility and energy' were the sort of positives to use.

Then we were given lunch in a separate dining room where we politely talked to one another leaving unsaid that one or other of us may get the job offer at the expense of another. Given the relative attraction of the positions and environment I am surprised it was thought safe for us to be all put together in the same room and given cutlery!

We were told to reassemble at two o'clock so there was time for a short walk on the seafront. Passing several appealing pubs I found out that I wasn't the only one that was attracted by the idea of a morale boosting liquid but we wisely resisted.

The afternoon session started with us being told that we were to be interviewed one at a time and when called we were to bring our bags and any coats etc with us. I imagine that this was so the dejected or triumphant weren't seen by the others waiting their turn, at least that seemed to be the plan.

I was called in quite quickly to meet the Head of Training again and the Company Secretary and Board member and after a couple of questions about my CV and the questionnaire I was told that I was going to be offered one of the positions. My relief and joy was such that I didn't really listen to the next sentence or two and when I recovered I seemed to remember something about the district office in Felixstowe being mentioned . I mumbled something about had I heard correctly as I thought Felixstowe was in East Anglia, outside their area as I had learned that their area only went as far north as South London. There was momentary confusion, both sides of the table while I think they were momentarily checking my A-level geography grade and maybe wondering whether English counties were outside the socioeconomics of the Welsh examination board.

For my part I recovered enough to say - sorry, you said Folkestone, near Dover in Kent. This must have provided reassurance and we shook hands and I was told to return to the Personnel Office where I would be given further details. I went down the corridor and stairs resisting a strong temptation to cheer and clap myself, (I hadn't heard anyone else doing this so it would perhaps appear rude.)

I had secure gainful, full time employment at what seemed to be a generous salary at least compared to a student grant. The fact that it wasn't to be in Brighton but in a place I had only vaguely heard of and never visited failed to take the edge of my

euphoria.

Folkestone

Some weeks later, early in November I found myself one dark November Sunday night booked into some random small hotel in Folkestone waiting to start my full time career. The next morning after a fortifying hotel breakfast I walked the few hundred yards from the hotel to the address on my appointment letter, York House, Cheriton Gardens.

As you can see from the two photos these offices were considerably smaller and less grand than the head offices in Hove where my interview took place but it was here that I was to start my career. The appointment letter stated I was to report at 9a.m. To Mr Yates, the District Administrative Officer, so at about ten to nine, anxious not to be late on my first day, I was ringing the doorbell on the heavy wooden front door. Then I went into a large, panelled hall with a wide staircase leading up out of it and several doors off it. After a few seconds a lady appeared, carrying a notebook and pen and asked me what I wanted. I gave her my name and said that I had been told to ask for Mr Yates. She wrote something down and went through one of the doors. After a few minutes she came back and asked me to take a seat on the of the hall chairs. I did so and as she didn't return I picked up and started to read the morning paper on the table next to me. A further ten minutes or so passed and a couple of people came in and rang a small bell near one of the doors which seemed to produce someone from behind one of the doors, sometimes papers and money was handed over, thanks given and the papers returned after a short interval. I hoped that I wasn't going to have to pay to see anyone as I had understood the transaction to work the other way i.e. I would turn up and money would eventually be given me. After another few minutes the original lady returned and offered me a cup of tea or coffee which I accepted. A few people passed through the hallway who I recognised as fellow workers as they were carrying papers and weren't wearing outdoor coats. They all seemed busier and to be working harder than I was, some of them said good morning and others just glanced at me as if they should know me but didn't. I recalled at the interview they talked about management training so consoled myself that if some of this comprised reading the paper and drinking coffee I had already acquired these skills and I was still getting paid. Eventually, the coffee provider returned and said that Mr Yates couldn't see me this morning but someone else would be coming to see me shortly. I suppressed my disappointment but thought it best not to throw a tantrum and leave demanding that they contact me at my hotel when he was available to me. Instead I thanked her and went back to finishing the paper. For a time I alternated between finishing the more boring sections in the paper that I had skipped over earlier and smiling broadly at other members of staff that I was beginning to think of as my colleagues judging that positive first impressions are always good.

Inside my head I was starting to imagine conversations starting all over the building along the lines of 'I wonder who the smartly dressed bearded young man in reception is and what does he want?' Or possibly 'who does that grinning loony in reception think he is sitting there reading the paper - it's not a library, someone should throw him out.' I had just started to interact with the public by telling those ringing the bell, who I had worked out could be paying their bills, that someone would be out to help them shortly and wondering why they didn't already have someone sitting there to perform this service. I was wondering whether this sort of creative thinking was just what the overlords back at Head Office had been hoping for when recruiting these keen minded graduate trainees. Luckily my daydreaming was broken as I was just starting to think this sitting down in a warm room after a large breakfast was making me sleepy, there were an improbable number of storage radiators in reception. Well it was the electricity board and they probably didn't pay for the electricity, (this was actually true!) when a smiling man came down the stairs. He introduced himself as Jeff, the Administration head and invited me to follow him to his office upstairs. Once there he offered coffee which I refused as it would be my fourth cup, having drunk two at breakfast and it wasn't yet ten o'clock. He explained that Mr Yates was away on a week's holiday and not at home with no means of being contacted. His deputy, who was at one of the electricity board shops that morning, knew nothing about me so could I explain what I wanted. My thoughts were that this didn't seem to be the switched-on, fast moving organisation that had been mentioned only a few weeks ago in Hove but wisely resisted saying so. The best plan seemed to be to show him my letter so I did and I think he found this helpful. He announced he would get on the phone to Head office and speak to me again after that but in the meantime would I mind going with him to another office where I could be found something useful to do. I was led downstairs to an office on the ground floor, labelled Registry on the door. Opening it, I followed my new namesake inside where I was met by two smiling ladies and two young girls who giggled behind their hands when I was introduced as Mr Dendle and they were told that I would be helping them today although the acting skills of any of them weren't sufficiently developed to hide their disbelief at this notion.

Jeff left me with them and I was introduced to them individually and quickly asked that they call me Geoff otherwise I would be constantly thinking they were addressing my Dad. The supervisor of this group, a tall young lady who I judged to be a few years older than me, (though I had already learned to never articulate any age related comment about ladies, even in the 1970's,) introduced herself as Lynn and asked what I was doing there. When I told her and said I had been interviewed at head office and said my arrival seemed to be something of a surprise to everyone, she gave a knowing smile and said "well head office is quite a long way from here." She explained that they had in the past recruited what they called clerical trainees straight from school and they often started their training with her as the function of the Registry was a combination of a sorting and distribution centre for post and other documents then a repository for these in a filing system as a sort of office library. If I wouldn't mind helping with this she was sure that in a day or two things would sort out and I discover what I was really there for. Meanwhile, as it was now tea break time the important matter of what I would like to drink and eat needed settling. It was explained there was a trolley with cakes, pastries, sandwiches and biscuits and although still full from breakfast I judged it important to fully immerse myself in the tribal routines of the office and settled on a Kit-Kat chocolate biscuit to accompany my coffee.

After this I was introduced into the mysteries of the filing and archives system some of which was housed in a series of large basement rooms and realised what a paper based organisation this was, as was typical at that time. Another function they performed was meeting the weekly stationery requests from the departments and it was explained that there was another similar sized office in the town as well as a couple of satellite depot offices across their area as well as seven shops. All of this was starting to help flesh out the organisation I had so recently joined. Later that afternoon Jeff came to see me and found me sorting piles of correspondence alphabetically before filing it away. We joked together that happily, although I had been born in Wales, English was my first language and I was thoroughly grounded in the alphabet and I confessed that I couldn't really speak any Welsh. He apologised and said that he would be busy at pre-arranged meetings the next day but was expecting some papers relating to the graduate training scheme to arrive from head office and he had cleared the following day to spend with me. I happily agreed and being a relatively organised person explained that I had enjoyed the afternoons filing and was being well looked after by my new colleagues.It's hard to remember that papers in those days needed conveying physically across the south coast by the Post Office, or in this case, I discovered by Securicor courier, no instant email or fax.

49

The next day was a full day of filing and the ladies made use of my youth and strength to move some of the heavier filing boxes around in the archives even finding a long butchers style apron to protect my new suit trousers which I was grateful for. That second lunchtime was my first chance in daylight to take half an hour to walk into the town centre, find the branch of my bank, in those days cash machines were much scarcer and I think you had to use the one for your particular bank. I also took my first look at the English Channel from the high vantage point of the Lees, a coastal parkland/promenade behind the high street and above the seafront. I could even see the French coast in the distance but the rest of the town centre and the harbour would have to explored another time. The filing was calling me. The next morning Jeff was waiting for me in reception "Come with me, I need to do something first, then we are going out." I followed him to a room where there was a wall of pigeon holes above a large desk on which was a stack of letters and packages, three or four large square courier cases and a pile of strong plastic style zipped document folders. He explained that every morning one of the section heads took responsibility for completing the first sort of post and documents from Head Office and the other depots and shops in the district. Every day the Securicor courier also brought output of data, documents and computer tabulations produced and printed at the data centre in Worthing known as the Central Accounts Office. He explained proudly that this district, South Kent was one of fourteen and in area the largest with the greatest length of overhead network which was more of a headache for his engineering colleagues but you will hear all about that in due course. I watched him for some forty minutes sorting and at last he said "Right we'll have a drive around the district and we can talk in the car." As he had described the district as large he explained we would only see a part of it today as the district stretched along the East Kent coast from the town of

Deal in the north through the Romney Marsh to the pretty town of Rye in the south and also contained the only nuclear power station in Seeboard at Dungeness, owned and operated at the time by the CEGB (the Central Electricity Generating Board.) I was already thinking that the business liked acronyms when Jeff who must have been reading my mind said, "you are too young to have been conscripted into the services?" He was right as it ceased in 1960 and I was far too young. He went on to say when the nationalised electricity industry was established in the late 1940's many of the senior staff were ex-service and their time in the forces had allowed them to develop an unhealthy enthusiasm for initials and acronyms and this seemed to have persisted as I would find out.

Changing the subject he said that a memo had arrived from Hove for him that morning which was a copy of a possible training outline devised by the HEO training and sent to each DAO for use with their graduate trainee. He then translated that the Higher Executive Officer (Training) had sent to the District Administrative Officer and this was when I started to enter into the spirit of things and asked whether as a graduate trainee if I was their 'GT' which I thought sounded suitably racy and yes, fast track. "No !" He answered curtly.
(It was to be some time before I was allowed to make up my own acronyms for the organisation but boy would I have some fun when I could !)
The day was interesting and not just because of the new acronyms I was acquiring. We visited a large stores and depot on the outskirts of Folkestone which Jeff admitted the managerial responsibility for was one if the bugbears of his job particularly when it included turning out at night to meet the police on site when an alarm was triggered. Often it was a fox, owl or stray cat but the valuable contents of tools and equipment meant there had been real robberies and attempts. I made a large mental note to avoid any

similar role to Jeff's in my future career, even at this early stage i.e. day 3, I was starting to map out a course. We went onto an electricity substation site where engineering staff were doing manly things with cranes and improbably large pieces of metal and wires. I was introduced to the engineer who was managing the process and who issued us with hard hats and advised us to keep well out of the way, advice that was unnecessary in my case as this all looked very skilled and dangerous. Reassuringly he met my preconceived ideas by having a rich Scottish accent and when Jeff told him I was a new graduate trainee, (I wasn't surprised that he resisted using my catchier GT acronym given his earlier reaction,) I was asked where I had read my engineering degree. My answer of joint honours in Economics and International Politics in a Welsh university had him red faced and spluttering and we didn't talk much after that and we left to go somewhere else. This view that the world revolved around engineering in my industry was a recurring theme.

We went on to visit two shops, one a large busy town centre in Ashford where afterwards we found a cafe for lunch. We then crossed back over the district to drive down through Hythe and south along the coast road and into the Romney Marsh. The coast was very different from the large, wide sandy beaches of my home town and seemed to be a narrow stretch of shingle punctuated by groins and breakwaters. The marsh itself was a strange landscape, very flat and grazed by many sheep and broken up by many ditches and drainage canals. There were a number of small isolated hamlets and villages, some on slightly raised pieces of land and often clustered around small squat medieval churches, some Jeff said were Saxon.

Jeff was good company and a fund of local knowledge describing himself as 'a man of Kent,' which meant he had been born and brought up in the county.

He explained that the Romney marsh in earlier centuries was more prone to flooding and the villages could often be cut off from one another. In earlier times regular church going was an essential part of life so even the smallest of settlements had built their own churches. I explained that this was a parallel to rural Wales except that there it would be a chapel in the settlement. He asked me whether I had gone to chapel and I believe that I surprised him by saying that I didn't think I had ever been inside one for a service although for two years in junior school one was used as an overflow classroom near the school. I went on to explain that my Mum was English and we went to a C of E church and she had in fact been born in Chatham. He seemed impressed both by the acronym and the Kent connection but judged it was time to talk of more delicate matters. He explained that the Head Office had said they had sent some papers to Mr Yates and there had been a discussion about the form the training would take and Jeff had to admit to them he hadn't got access to these so they had reluctantly sent a copy. He also admitted that he hadn't owned up to them that my arrival had been a surprise and thought it best not too. I tried to lighten the mood and said 'Well, we are quite a long way from Hove.' He gave me an old fashioned look and said - "You seem to be a quick learner," then laughed and said "I think we will have a new start Monday when all should be clearer. Until then we should be able to manage another day out and the rest of the time we'll hide you in filing."

We drove onto a much smaller shop in the village of New Romney where the shop manager seemed pleased to see us and quickly offered us coffee and biscuits. He told us this afternoon was quiet as there had been a market that morning and people had combined their shopping with it and at this time of the year many of his customers hurried home before dusk. He also explained the 'social' nature that his shop supplied because everyone has electricity bills that can be paid in the shop and some of his customers save up towards them by buying electricity savings stamps, something I was unaware of as we hadn't used them in my family.

"We benefit with some shop sales because we have no competitors locally for appliances, people would have to travel to Ashford, Folkestone or even Hastings. We also make sales to the CEGB workers at Dungeness power station because they get staff discount from us."

This was news to me and it was explained that I was entitled to this and could buy goods at cost price plus 5 %. I started to cast my eyes over the display of portable TV's and stereos and also thought as I liked to get a bargain I knew where my Xmas shopping would be done that year. After we left Jeff pointed out some dark square blocks in the distance and told me that was Dungeness Power Station and its size was obvious as I was told we were still almost ten miles away from it.

I spent the next day in filing but someone from personnel called down and went through some helpful admin stuff such as bank details to pay in my salary and tax and National insurance arrangements. The also gave me details of some letting agents when I mentioned that I needed to look for a flat. In conversation I mentioned that I was from Wales which surprised them and they commented on my lack of a Welsh accent and that I wasn't called Jones. I was also asked if I found Folkestone to be busy after coming from Wales. There were a few comments like this over the coming weeks which maybe showed that people at that time were less well travelled. Anyway, my stock reply was 'well not really, my home town had 200,000 people, about the size of Brighton but with better beaches.' The next day Jeff arranged we would go out and see a bit more of the district and when I told him I was looking for a flat we drove around Folkestone and its suburbs to give me a better idea of the local areas. Folkestone is quite spread out with some hilly areas and although I liked the look of some of the suburbs I was beginning to think it would make sense to live near the office and the town centre, at least until I bought a car. We visited the other office in the town centre, a large three storey building above the shop in the High Street where the Engineering and Commercial departments were based. Engineering included their drawing office as well a network control centre where I was told that faults and outages on the network was managed. Thankfully, we avoided any new conversations about my chosen degree course. The commercial department was all about selling wiring and heating services to customers.The best thing about the office was the view out the back over the sea and the French coast visible in the distance.

Jeff suggested that if I wanted to visit a couple letting agents maybe they could arrange some early viewings for me, perhaps at the weekend to avoid a longer stay in the hotel. The first agent I went to had a few interesting small flats and I explained that I would prefer something central near to the office and town. One or two caught my eye and one that was vacant was next to a park and within walking distance of the office. I arranged a viewing for the end of the week in my lunch hour so pleased with the success I met up again with Jeff to continue our tour. After a quick lunch we drove out of Folkestone and headed north to Dover. The afternoon was spent calling into the two shops in Dover and Deal further up the coast as well as visiting the Training Centre outside Dover where we saw some engineering apprentices practicing on dummy overhead lines and trenches as well as a well-equipped workshop.
Nearing the end of my first week I was coming to the conclusion that I had joined a large and complex organisation that seemed to be full of busy people who knew what they were doing as was evidenced by the lights continuing to work both indoors and in the street. Unless I was to follow a career based around filing, which I felt that I had mastered, I wondered

how long it would take for me to make some sense of it all and more importantly to find a role in the organisation which I could carry off with a degree of confidence and be useful enough to justify continued employment and a salary!

Still, of greater immediate importance was finding somewhere to live as the initial novelty of living in a hotel, albeit one with cooked breakfasts and palatable evening meals was starting to wear off.

The next day was a Friday, the end of my first week at work and after a busy morning, yes ...filing, I left the office and walked the short distance around the corner where the agent met me outside a large Victorian semi-detached house.

I followed him upstairs where a second panelled front door opened into the flat.

It was basically two rooms and a bathroom, all off a narrow hall. The bedroom was large and the living room had a kitchen corner in it but nice views out to the south with the view of the town bisected by a railway viaduct which was interesting. The furniture all seemed serviceable and the flat was clean with the living room quite light although I realised for a couple of months I would mostly be seeing it in the dark, at least on weekdays and I only saw it as a short term alternative to the hotel until I found something better. My overwhelming feeling was this all seemed very grown up, particularly now I had a permanent job. At university in my first year I had stayed in digs with a family who provided cooked breakfasts and weekend meals and in the second and third years I shared a purpose built student flat and although we cooked our meals in a shared kitchen/diner there was a cleaner for the common areas and I lived in a study/bedroom. Here I was the other end of the country from my home town and familiar friends and places, in a strange town, working with strangers in a totally new environment after three years in a small university town living with friends in a setting that had seem familiar and comfortable. It wasn't so much the leaving home as I had spent a couple of happy months back with my parents but having left home for university at eighteen I was pretty independent and wanted a home of my own but the new environment of a new job in a strange town far away from familiar people felt as isolated as any time in my life. My then girlfriend had already started a college course in Kingston on Thames a couple of hours away by train and in those days of limited communication contact was either by letter or by synchronised phone calls to a phone box and was not yet sure about personal phone calls at the office, particularly as I didn't yet have my own desk let alone a phone extension!

My first weekend in my new town consisted of a walk along the promenade on a cold and dark Friday evening before eating an evening meal back at the hotel sitting by myself at a table reading the local paper.

Saturday was more promising as I went into the letting agent and signed up as a tenant for the flat that I had viewed and I was pleased to hear that I could pick up the keys at the start of the week so I only had two more nights at the dreary hotel. This galvanised me as I knew I need to buy bedding and other essentials although I wasn't exactly sure what as I hadn't fully taken in what equipment the furnished flat came with.

In town I bought some bedding and mugs, glasses and cutlery from the local department store, Bobby's which I discovered had a good cafe upstairs. To get to it you passed a pianist playing a baby grand piano on the spacious landing. It was like going back in time in a P G Wodehouse story. I thought I would work out what else I needed after I got the keys. I found I could leave my purchases in the store while I explored the town further and discovered a water powered vehicular railway (if that's the right term,) which went from the cliff top on the Lees down to the lower promenade next to the beach. There had been one in Aberystwyth so it made me feel more at home. From the prom you could walk below the cliffs to the harbour and from there return back to the town centre on a windy cobbled street with seaside type gift shops and small galleries including a Rock shop where you could watch sticks of rock being made including the lettering before the warm sticky mixture was stretched out back and forth before being cut into sticks for sale. I had never seen this process before so this was new. I went into the Seeboard shop and admired the small TV's but when I asked to see the staff price my lack of a Staff ID card that I was yet to receive caused something of a dilemma to the sales woman. Luckily the shop manger appeared and recognised me from the visit earlier in the week and agreed to show the discounts although they would need my staff ID details for a purchase. I explained that I would come back once I was in my new flat as I may be needing other appliances.

Monday morning I was back at the office when a smiling grey haired man came into Registry and after introducing himself as Mr Yates said that he owed me an apology and would I come up with him to his office for a chat. This seemed promising as he was my new boss and I already had him at a disadvantage, I knew this needed careful handling. His office was large and nicely furnished with wood panelling and what seemed like a lot of furniture and it contrasted strongly with the rooms I had been in so far which seemed more utilitarian with furniture that didn't seem to match. The room also had framed paintings and a large map of Kent on the wall with the district boundary marked and little coloured pins for the depots, offices and shop. Large matching panelled bookcases filled one wall with shelves of labelled files filling them. I was invited to sit in one armchair in a bay window and he sat down in the other with a coffee table between us with a bone china coffee set on a tray, rather different from the plastic cups I had been drinking out of from the vending machine the previous week. The whole office looked very organised so I was surprised when he said again "I owe you an apology, last week was completely my fault. I had the wrong Monday in my diary so I was expecting you to start today." I thought it best not to embarrass him any further so I said I had been well looked after in his absence and had sorted out a number of things including somewhere to live.

"So what did you do last week?"

I thought I would need to present the week in the best possible light, for the sake of everyone involved including present company.

'The Admin head was very helpful in arranging visits for me to see the other offices, stores and depots. We also visited some shops and he sorted out some letting agents do that I could find a flat but he said you would be dealing with the arrangements for my training programme when you returned and he didn't want to interfere with that.

Looking puzzled he said, "where did you spend the rest of the week though?"

I tried my best but all I could think to say was, 'Well, Lynn in Registry had a lot of filing and archiving to do so I helped with that.'

Spluttering, he put down his coffee cup and getting rather red-faced he blurted out -"That's where we start the sixteen year old school leavers ! If Head Office hear we've had one of their new graduate trainees doing our filing I'll never hear the end of it - you're supposed to be following a well structured training course!"

Then it went very quiet and I tried to think of something constructive to say and dismissed my first thought of 'I won't tell them if you don't' for the more factual statement of 'Well, Head Office is a long way from here.'

I am not sure it was the best thing I could have said as he replied with

"I see you have been listening to some of my staff last week - I would also say bad news travels fast - and a long way. But anyway let's put last week behind us." He went over to his desk and came back with a thin file of papers. Opening it up he explained that for some time there had been discussion at Board level of instituting a programme to bring in future potential senior staff for the organisation from outside the engineering profession. He explained that this had been a struggle as the Board Chairman and several other board members were professional engineers and needed convincing that such a move was necessary and indeed helpful. Concerted pressure from the Chief Accountant, Board Secretary and others had finally won and the concession was that a small group of non-engineering graduates were recruited and I was one of these.

So if I understood it correctly, I was part of an experiment and I could see that telling Head Office that one of their experimental 'bright young things' had almost mastered filing was not going to convince them that the long term future of the organisation had been secured!

I sensed he was anxious to put any discussion about last week to bed and poured more coffee for us and kindly asked where I had found to live and when I explained it was a small flat a short distance away from the office and opposite Radnor Park he said that he understood that was a good part of town and to let him know if I needed any assistance with anything. I remembered the ID card needed for shop purchases and he said of course Personnel can sort that out today, they will need to take your photo for it.

Having recovered from the shock he opened the slim file of papers and looking at the first page said "it's important to realise that the new graduate intake has been given a high priority by the Board", (I was to discover that the use of the term 'the Board' as well as referring to the board of directors also was commonly used as shorthand for the organisation.) "Myself and my fellow district Amin Officers or DAO's as we are known, have with Head Office training developed a programme to be followed over your first two years." (the love of all businesses for acronyms meant that they were referred to generally as DAO's - many years later I discovered that DAO is a Portuguese wine region and the name appears prominently on wine bottles. If only I had known that then or maybe one of his fine wooden cabinets already contained a stock of these bottle -perhaps I would find out at Xmas if relations between us remained cordial.)

He went on to say that to reflect the importance placed on the initiative the Graduate trainees, (hmm..was this the time for me to introduce my GT term? - probably not,) had been put on accelerated grades, so our grade and salary would be one normally used for a section head or supervisor. The relatively high starting salary, which I must admit had been an attraction to me, meant they'd attracted good quality candidates and had been able to select the best from this field.

I have since read that it is an accepted selection technique to say this and encourages competition between recruits by making them feel good about their abilities whilst at the same time perhaps discouraging complacency because you feel you need to maintain your performance levels because of the high abilities of the others, while you are doubting your own abilities. One term I have heard is 'imposter syndrome,' I was yet to suffer from it but it was only the start of week two.

He also warned that there was a fear expressed that there might be some resentment felt in some quarters over the appointments given that in the past people would 'work their way up,' and a grade 5, if I remember it correctly, was something to aspire to and could be the pinnacle of some careers.

61

"Anyway", he went on, "it was only something to be aware of."

He then outline the plans for the graduate trainees to spend some time in as many of the departments in the district as possible over the two year period but often this could be in a junior, hands-on role to learn how the departments functioned. I privately thought this sounded a bit like last week's filing and maybe he hadn't needed to get so excited. He also said that the district offices were experiencing staff shortages in some roles with trained staff being attracted to some of the new offices in the area of finance, insurance, healthcare and travel companies who were offering 'fringe benefits' such as cheap mortgages and insurance. I privately thought you would need to buy a lot of staff price toasters and batteries to compete with those benefits. The advantage for me is many of those departments would be short staffed so would be likely to welcome an extra pair of hands, even one with an inflated salary, although he said that the cost for us was currently on Head Offices budget so my labour was effectively free. (So hopefully good value - I thought.)

I was also given some more welcome news, particularly as I would now become responsible for my own groceries and cooking once I left the hotel, the training would begin with a one week residential induction course. This would be held at North Frith, a country house near Tonbridge owned by Seeboard and it would take place in a week's time. He also explained that I would need to catch the train to Tonbridge which was a separate town to Tunbridge Wells. This was news to me as I was aware of the latter, as in the cliche 'furious of Tunbridge Wells,' but the other Tonbridge was unknown to me but after the recent Felixstowe / Folkestone fiasco at the interview I kept quiet, although I did wonder if this stealing and misspelling of their town's name may be contributing to the legendary ill-temper of the good citizens of Tunbridge Wells.

It was then explained that I would start in one of the departments straight away, I was to graduate from the world of filing, but before that he wanted to introduce me to the other acronyms in the management team. There would be a DCE (commercial,) a DE (engineering) and the acronym of DM i.e the district manager. On the way we called in on a lady who was the secretary to all of them and who was possibly responsible for ensuring they didn't get their Monday's muddled up. I thought it prudent to not mention this and instead said to all of them how pleased I was to be here and get away from all that useless studying of Economics and Politics, (I didn't actually say that but I had been warned that all three were engineers and might ask why I wasn't an engineering graduate.)
In fact, they all were very welcoming, interested that I had come all the way from Wales and wished me well. I did notice that they all had nicely furnished offices. The manager said I would be invited to sit in on some of his management meetings as part of my training and if I had been more deluded I would already be imagining sitting in one of them within a matter of weeks but back to reality. I was allocated to Debt Collection which pretty much did 'what it said on the tin.' When I was taken through the door off the reception hall I recognised it as the door through which people emerged to take cash, cheques and papers from the customers who had come into reception only last week when I had sat there waiting.

I was left with the section head who seemed friendly and said call me Bob so I guess that was his name. The office was a panelled room on the ground floor with a bay window and a huge fireplace on one wall which had a large safe where the grate had been. I daydreamed that if it was my office I would put a grate back in and make toast and cook crumpets there but was brought back to reality by realising Bob had been indicating the names of his colleagues and I

63

had missed the first couple. I reasoned that I would be there for long enough to learn their names so thought it impolite to ask him to repeat them and just grinned inanely at each of them in turn. It appeared that although Bob had been told of my arrival it could only have been earlier that morning and his brief introduction to the rest of the office that this Mr Dendle had been appointed from Head Office and would be spending a few weeks with them seemed, judging by their puzzled expressions, to raise more questions than answers. In case they knew I came from Wales I thought I had better say something, in English so I managed a 'please call me Geoff.' Just then the secretary from upstairs came in and said that Personnel were ready for me upstairs so I followed her out of the room, hearing a hubbub of conversation from my new colleagues in the room behind me as the door closed. I imagine it was something along the lines of "who is that bearded spy from Head Office and what has he got to grin about." I just hope that nobody told them my grade and salary details. Upstairs I was shown into a small office where a middle aged man and a younger man nearer my own age sat at two desks facing one another. They introduced themselves as the personnel manager Percy and his assistant Nigel.

Their office was furnished in a similar style to Registry downstairs and certainly lacked any oil paintings or panelling. They explained that some administrative stuff was needed, Nigel would arrange my ID card and there was some forms to fill in about tax, national insurance etc and they needed my bank details so I could be paid. They even offered me a salary advance if I needed it which seemed generous and unexpected. I was able to give them my new address in the flat although I explained I hadn't moved in yet and hoped to do that lunchtime. Helpfully they offered to help me move my possessions and Nigel said he could do it in one of the couriers vans. I thanked them but told them it wasn't necessary as I only had two bags and

64

the flat was nearby and only a few doors from the hotel. After we sorted out the forms I was told they knew that I would be going on a course at the Staff training college next week and they would arrange a rail warrant for the tickets and I also needed to call and collect my daily allowance money for the week. Puzzled, I said that I understood that meals were provided there. Amused by this I was told the allowance was in effect for drinks in the bar each evening - privately, I thought this just gets better and better.

I returned to the debt collection office downstairs where I sat with Bob for an hour where he outlined the activities that went on. Although we had electricity at home for all my life I had no awareness of accounts and payments but thinking about it I could see there was a flaw in the arrangements as generally you paid in arrears after your usage was calculated. Perhaps I had led a sheltered life. I had assumed everyone paid their electricity bills but this room full of eight or nine people seemed to suggest otherwise. He explained that consumer (not customer!) records were held on computer files at the Central Accounts Office in Worthing, (known of course as CAO.) It was here that meter readings and payment information was sent to update the records with paper updates in the form of account records being sent to the district offices as well as any details of overdue accounts that were unpaid after the customer had received the bill, followed by the reminder. For those unpaid accounts Notices of Disconnection letters were sent to the district with a paper record which was filed in the office to record subsequent follow up action. I was of course delighted to discover in the wealth of organisational acronyms I was learning that these were called NOD's or in an attempt to make an unpleasant action more friendly - 'Noddies.'

I took the lunch break to collect the flat key after arranging to meet the letting agent at the flat and also collected my few possessions from the nearby hotel. There wasn't much time to completely absorb the features of my new home but I could see the furnished flat contained enough to allow cooking etc. But it still seemed a little strange and perhaps a bit lonely, although I was glad to see it in daylight as I knew it would be dark after work. Anyway it was time to go back to the office and the 'Land of Nods.'

Bob handed me over to his assistant who seemed a bit formal and introduced himself by his surname, nevertheless he knew a lot about Debt Collection and explained that there were 'live accounts' where the debtor was still at the premises and 'closed accounts' where the debtor had moved and was either at a new premises or was being traced for action through the courts. The sequence was explained where the initial quarterly account, (for households and small businesses,) was followed some four weeks later by a reminder letter, then ten days later by a disconnection letter which was referred to this office for action before the Notice (recorded on the NOD) was issued to one of our 'Cut off men' to go to the customer's premises. They would either receive payment on the door or could, as a last resort, disconnect the supply inside the house.

There were all sorts of complications which he touched on and some of which I understood, for example larger business premises were billed monthly. In bad weather such as snow, disconnections were suspended, magistrates warrants could be obtained to enter premises and some disconnections could be made outside as a last resort, by digging up the pavement or road and cutting the cable. This was rare and cost the customer a larger reconnection fee to be re-supplied. I realised there was a whole world here that I had previously been totally unaware of. My belief we lived in a law- abiding civilised country had not included the possibility of people digging up roads to cut off electricity to homes. I was beginning to see the use of the term 'consumers' of electricity in preference to 'customers' which implied a contractual arrangement where a supply was paid for!

It was also explained that calls were taken from customers who had disputes over non-payment and would phone to say a cheque was in the post or all sorts of other excuses which seemed to be of 'the dog ate my homework variety.' Sometimes the phone call or a face to face conversation with the customer would result in negotiated payment arrangements of instalments or post-dated cheques. There was also the option of giving customers a coin operated prepayment meter so that they managed their payments but I was later to discover this was no panacea. I was told that I would be involved in some of the paper handling before being unleashed on the phones or negotiations and it didn't look like I would be called on to knock on any doors or dig up any cables any time soon, which was a great relief.

Going back to my new flat that evening seemed a lonely experience as there had at least been some other guests at the hotel to at least say good evening to and a TV and bar to use. In all honesty after all these years I don't have a very strong memory of the flat or living there. I guess I must have cooked evening meals there sometimes but maybe I ate main meals at lunch time. I had only used an electric cooker at the student flat and I think it was the same here and I think the heating was by storage radiators so I guess I was showing some solidarity with my new employers. I had a radio but had already decided to buy a small tv and exercise my right to staff discount at an early opportunity. There wasn't a phone in the flat or a shared one in the hallway so calls to my girlfriend at college in Kingston on Thames were difficult although it wasn't long before I established that personal calls could be taken at the office which made things easier.

Staff College

The graduate induction course was the first opportunity to meet other graduate trainees and compare notes and I wondered whether any of the other successful recruits had been some of the ones I had lunched with those weeks back at the interview day. The day started early and I had been told that there would be someone at Tonbridge station to pick me up and take me to the college. Good as their word a man was standing at the exit gate of the station holding a large 'Seeboard Staff College' sign. He showed me to a minibus and explained that there was another train due in ten minutes bringing two others for the course. Once they had been collected we drove a few miles north of Tonbridge and eventually through large gates past a lodge and up a long driveway lined by tall, mature trees. We parked at the end of the drive where there stood a huge red brick and tile hung house, like a stately home, this looked promising. We were welcomed by a smart military looking man who introduced himself as the warden of the college and

said we would be shown our rooms shortly but led us

into a large room he described as the library and indeed there were several bookcases but also a lot of comfortable armchairs but what caught my eye was the view out of one of the several large, floor to ceiling bay windows. A large manicured lawn led down to a huge lake with golden leaved trees on the opposite bank beautifully reflected in the dark water. Our welcomer announced that the lake was the original reservoir for Tonbridge but now was a well-stocked fishing lake for use of Seeboard staff, I regretted that my fishing tackle was still at my parent's house or I assumed it was as I hadn't used it since the age of fifteen or sixteen.

It was suggested we helped ourselves to teas or coffees while he went off to find the earlier arrivals who were somewhere being shown around. My two companions from the station had travelled down from Surrey and the Medway towns and we all seemed very impressed with what we had seen so far but equally were unsure about what the coming week would hold. We compared notes on what we had been told back at our offices but concluded that no-one there had a much better idea than we did and the term 'Graduate Induction course' seemed suitable vague. The other three 'inductees' were returned to the library and explained that in the last half an hour they had seen the dining room next door, the lecture rooms and been walked around some of the grounds where they had been shown the tennis court, croquet lawn, boathouse, the walled kitchen garden where much of the fresh food was grown and most interestingly the bar and games room across the courtyard in the Orangery where there were snooker and bar billiards tables. It seemed like the week's course would be tolerable whatever the induction was about. The three other course members were a trainee from the data centre who said she was a trainee programmer, another district trainee from Surrey and a trainee assigned to Head Office in the Secretary's department who despite where he worked was quick to declare he had as much knowledge about the week as the rest of us although he did offer the fact that there were sixteen graduate trainees on the programme in total and we were on the first induction course.

Before we could chat any more we were invited across the hallway, a dark panelled room with a heavy winding staircase going up past a series of framed portraits, into one of the lecture rooms which had more modern decor and lighting, set up with desks and whiteboards and a projector screen where we were welcomed by the warden and the Head of Training who had been on the interview panel. We were given housekeeping information and some history about the house and grounds which we discovered was earlier owned by the Hornes clothing family and before the house was built in 1889 the estate was a hunting estate dating back to pre-Tudor times. Then the philosophy behind the recruitment of graduates outside the engineering discipline was described. It seemed the organisation was anticipating the coming years to be a period of greater innovation in business and was looking towards such recruitments as a way of developing more professional skills and a greater ability to innovate in the organisation. It felt that a weight of expectation was being placed on our shoulders and it was outlined that training courses like this week would be a regular part of training with emphasis on skills such as presentation and supervisory and management training.

The passage of time has meant that the details of the week are lost to me, the details of North Frith are much clearer but then over the years I spent more time there so it must have refreshed my memories. What I do remember is a series of talks from senior members of staff giving details of their functions and of being very impressed by their depths of knowledge and their professionalism.

A few years later I met one of the managers who had given a talk that week. He admitted feeling intimidated by speaking to us as we were previously described to him as being such a group of bright recruits; it's easy to forget that in those days the percentage of school leavers obtaining university degrees was nearer five percent not today's fifty percent. I also wonder whether our depth of ignorance and reluctance to show ourselves up in front of one another made us a more intimidating audience than, in reality, we were.

During the week we were inundated with information from senior managers from the whole range of disciplines and functions in the organisation. It was a strange mixture of intensive information gathering and very pleasant socialising in a wonderful privileged environment. The lecture sessions, for that was what was what the first few days comprised, were interspersed with strolls around the grounds, sociable chatting, games of snooker and plenty of good food and drink. I am sure I had gained a few pounds during the week but more importantly I had gained a few friends and a greater, if theoretical, knowledge of the organisation I was now part of. One interesting insight was the talk we were given by the company's head of legal services who dismissed the workings of the Debt Collection activity in a brief sentence. I felt slighted on behalf of my new colleagues of only a week having seen how dedicated they were in chasing debtors before the last resort of court action. He then went into great detail about the Legal process of chasing the unpaid debts through the courts and in that session

I gained a couple of valuable insights that I was to find very helpful throughout my career:-

Firstly, all workers have a particular viewpoint of their function in any organisation often to the detriment of others.

Secondly, pride in ones own contribution is essential and allows the best performance.

Thirdly, somewhere in any organisation it is essential to take a measured and systematic view over these 'hand offs' between functions and I wondered where this happened and who did it.

Fourthly, after initially laboriously scribbling notes down in the first day's sessions, as if there was going to be an exam at the end of the course, I decided I would just spend the sessions listening closely to the presenters and only jot down a key point I would try and find out about later or a question to ask at the end of the sessions

I was also becoming a silent critic of the presentations and trying to decide what approach I would attempt in their position. This was probably arrogant but we had been expected at university to give verbal presentations at seminars and tutorial groups so I had a little experience already. The time was before pc's and PowerPoint presentations but some of the talks used overhead projection or 35 mm slides.
As well as the lectures we were given some group work tasks towards the end of the week but I have no detailed memory of these.

One of the benefits of the week was that I exchanged phone numbers with the others and over the coming months it was interesting to compare notes with each other on how we were getting on back in our districts. On the last evening we walked down the quiet country lanes for a few farewell drinks in a nearby country pub that was recommended to us. The landlord recognised us as strangers and asked us if we had 'escaped' from the staff college which was amusing. As incarcerations go it was certainly a benevolent one and we vowed we would keenly sign up for any future courses going, although I pointed out that the overhead linesman course on a dummy set of towers that we had viewed in the grounds would be one I would be resisting. Over the years of my career I would spent more time at North Frith and as well as enjoying future courses I would later give lectures and run courses there. For a brief time, when I was feigning a financial and accounting expertise, I visited frequently from my day job at Head Office to monitor their spending and prepare their annual budget submissions. I also vaguely recall being phoned to ask if was interested in the position of Centre manager and warden which I quickly dismissed on health and waist-line grounds. This was all in the future but it was with some regret that we left at the end of the week to return to the reality of the day job.

A strange coincidence occurred recently. During the period of the pandemic lockdown I received, out of the blue, an email from a Mike Thomas asking me if I had gone to Sketty school and was expecting a birthday shortly, accurately stating the date of my birthday. It went on to explain that we had been in junior school together and he had a copy of a photo taken at my tenth birthday party. I remembered him as a close friend of that time who had gone on to a separate grammar school and shortly afterwards he had moved away because of his father's job. We subsequently met a couple of years later for one evening when his family were back in Swansea and I believe we went to the Castle cinema to see the first Beatles film which would have been at the age of thirteen in the summer of 1964.

After a number of phone conversations and daring to view each other on Zoom after a gap of almost sixty years we eventually managed to meet in Kent at Mike's house. We went out for lunch with our partners and spent a pleasant day in conversation during the course of which it was revealed that they had briefly lived in the penthouse flat of the converted North Frith house - spooky!

Training 'On the Job.'

The week after the North Frith course I was back in the office in the swing of debt collection. There was a distraction of a post course debrief with the DAO and Personnel head but the conversation centred around what I thought of the college and the catering, which was clearly the highlight of anyone's visit. There and also a short interrogation over how the other trainees were being deployed in their offices. I resisted telling them that none of the others had been given the solid grounding in filing that I had been able to acquire but instead said that the approach seemed similar to ours of assignment to a department with staffing needs and making themselves useful which they seemed satisfied with.

In debt collection with my new colleagues it was a similar story with any that had attended the college enthusiastic about the catering and the grounds and those who had never been, suppressing their envy. I thought it wise not to relay the good news I had been given that a few more visits to courses there would be part of my training. In contrast to the theory offered during my course I was now involved in more hands-on activity of paper sorting, checking records, taking payments and recording payment arrangements sent in by post, yes in those far off days people wrote letters to their electricity supplier!

I was also introduced to the records office where some dozen or so clerks had responsibility for some ten thousand customer records each and amazingly such was the staff continuity, or their powers of recall that they claimed to almost have a personal relationship with some customers. Rather different from the random impersonal contact of call centres today but some would say less efficient, it's hard to gauge. The records held details of whether there were health issues, access problems or even fierce dogs at

74

the household. It all seemed very personal. There were other interesting conversations with the 'cut off' men when they returned to the office late in the afternoon or the next morning. They brought back tales from the 'debt front line' and it seemed they also had personal knowledge of some of their customers, or strictly speaking, consumers. They were alert to twitching curtains or people hiding behind sofas and the oft told stories of the dog having eaten the bill (and the reminder and the follow up letter ?) and stories of the 'cheques in the post.' Though genial with us in the office there was a certainly an air of world weariness acquired from constant exposure to people with a casual relationship with the truth.

I do remember their frustration some mornings back in the office when any details had been passed through from engineering control over any disconnected supplies that had been reconnected due to a communication breakdown or particularly skilled storytelling on the part of the consumer. There seemed to be a tricky moral and administrative tightrope to walk in this.

The members of debt collection had a front-line mentality about them as if they were the last line of defence between the financial viability of the Board and the horde of lying scroungers out there in wider society. I am sure it wasn't that simple and there were schemes such a fuel direct payment from the DHSS and contacts form charities supporting ex-servicemen, Kent having garrison towns in this area. The would listen patiently to the various excuses given for non-payment and instalment arrangements were often made or referrals to other benefit agencies. In the weeks that followed I graduated to taking customer calls and negotiating and agreeing payment arrangements which seemed like quite a responsibility, that I didn't take lightly.

After some weeks I was told that it was time to move on and gain some experience of other departments. I think the plan was for me to work in Personnel and Admin but after only a couple of days I was told of a change of plan as they were short-staffed in the Engineering clerical section and my 'assistance' would be useful there. Given the cynicism my chosen academic discipline had been met with on my brief meeting with an engineer earlier I was not sure how I would be received. I needn't have worried as the section was managed by a kindly lady who tolerated the engineers but treated them with an unpredictable mixture of helpfulness and scolding and it was clear they often didn't know which treatment they would receive. I moved over to the office which was a large building on the High Street above the Seeboard shop with a view over the channel to the distant French coast. The location in the town centre was handy for any lunch time shopping. Marjorie welcomed my help and was quick to introduce me to a number of administrative tasks which she wasn't shy in saying were her least favourite duties. They were apparently a couple of staff short of the agreed staffing level so my presence was seen as being very welcome. The engineers themselves were a mixture of older guys in their fifties and early sixties who it seemed had been recruited when the networks were being expanded after the war. As well as these there were a few younger engineers nearer my own age.

There was a drawing office where network and substation plans were produced, a wayleaves group that was responsible for negotiating access for new lines across land and were distinguished by dressing like gentlemen farmers in corduroy and tweeds and had adopted rucksacks rather than brief cases for their papers. They would often come into the office with mud on their stout brogue shoes and get a semi-good natured scolding from Marjorie. She reserved the stronger scoldings for the younger engineers most of whom seemed actually quite fearful of her and already started to use me as a kind of go-between; dropping off their reports and claim forms to me once they

76

could see she was away from her desk with whispers of "could you put that in the In Tray and not tell her I just brought it now," then scuttling away before she returned. The thing that caused the most tension was the checking of expense claims and car allowance forms that were paid out either weekly or into the monthly salaries. Any queries and rejections could delay the payment and it was the task of the clerical staff to check their legitimacy.

It was interesting to see the network operation side of the business and the planning and construction engineers were patient in their briefings and explanations to me about their roles. I was shown the resource control scheduling systems, a wall board system with manually written cards planning the deployment in the weeks ahead for manpower and plant. All in all I could see it was a very professional organisation with people who took pride in correctly performing their roles with much talk of their responsibility for 'keeping the lights on for the people of Kent.'

I am not sure if it was planned but after a few weeks, including taking over the responsibility for the Resource planning for a week (and not hearing that the wrong number of men were in the wrong location on the wrong day, thankfully!) I was told that Marjorie would be away for a month and I was to act as temporary office manager. This seemed a bit sudden but it at least reduced any residual guilt I may have had about being overpaid. Her deputy, a man near my Dad's age, who seemed to specialise in the resource planning role was kind enough to say I could always ask him anything I needed to know. He was also kind enough to boost my confidence by saying I had done a good job covering for him on the resource planning so at least I knew there weren't teams of lost linesmen down in Romney Marsh due to my inexperience.

The month went well and I don't think there were any disasters even when I had to attend a management meeting representing the section. In fact the biggest crisis I remember was when a young, fat seagull fell onto one of the office window sills and flapped into and around the office and I was the one to catch him and release him onto the fire escape where the parents returned for him so I guess this was a demonstration of small scale crisis management. I think the hardest part was trying to ensure that everything was completed before the full timer returned. During the month I took the opportunity to phone a couple of the other graduates to see how they were getting on, and possibly to boast about my temporary elevation. It seemed that similar temporary positions had also been found for them so it did look as if the Board was serious about our future management prospects.

The next movement was different and said a lot in retrospect about 1970's business management and an insight into industrial relations in British industry at that time.

To my knowledge so called modern business practices along with junk food, cowboy films and Walt Disney had been imported from across the Atlantic in increasing quantities particularly since the invasion of the country by US troops prior to the Normandy Landings. Probably best not to debate the value of this as it doesn't seem to have stopped with us importing 'out of town retail parks',

Fast food joints, obesity (any connection?) and lots of other innovations of mixed merit. Large organisations in the UK embraced some of these revolutionary techniques coming over and were keen to worship at the altars of MIT, the Harvard Business school and the like. Seeboard operated two productivity schemes that were designed to reward efforts financially. To operate such schemes it is necessary to establish a norm of expected performance against which to measure actual performance. I heard a little on the induction course about a Head Office department called the Management Services Unit (of course it was known as

the MSU - remember the love of acronyms here.)
Amongst other exciting skills practiced by them such
as Operational Research and Regression Analysis most
of the staff worked at Work Study i.e. so they told me,
working out how long tasks took by watching them
-with a stopwatch to time them!
I was already familiar with a dangerous occupation in
the field with an industrial trade known as 'Cable
Watcher.' This sounds simple enough until you find out
it describes the activity of standing at the edge of a
trench or hole being dug by a JCB with the duty of
drawing the driver's attention a split second before his
metal shovel slices through a live cable and sends
11,000 volts through him and his JCB whilst at the
same time probably blowing the said cable watcher off
his feet! I concluded that sitting next to someone
working for hours on end while timing them with a
stop watch had the potential for a poke in the eye
with a pen at best and out in the field with shovels
and other implements to hand, the potential for
injuries of greater severity.
Anyway, Seeboard had fully embraced these schemes
and clerical workers were able to add a CWM (clerical
work measurement!) productivity payment equivalent
to some 5 % if their salary and I think from memory it
was a group scheme based on output of each small
group and again from memory it was generally
achieved so when I heard this I wondered several
things:
Firstly, were these scores of work study 'experts' and
their stopwatches a waste of time?

Secondly, Did they have any other skills than working
a stopwatch?

Thirdly, Maybe the standard performance measures
weren't ambitious enough?

Finally - How many of them had been subjected pen
based injuries?

Industrial staff (in the jargon of the time, blue collared workers,) had a productivity scheme but the engineers were considered to be above such scrutiny, they even had an association instead of a trade union. They were also paid, I found out, a responsibility allowance in lieu of a bonus scheme and although I agree network switching and building power lines needs responsible behaviour I had discovered meeting deadlines for their paperwork was often beyond their sense of responsibility.

All of this became less theoretical when I was asked to go and see Mr Yates after being told my time in Engineering clerical was due to come to an end. He said that they had been pleased with my covering for the section head and planned to continue with my rotation through the district departments. He then looked a bit uncomfortable and said the districts had been approached by MSU at Head Office to see if any of the graduate trainees would be interested in joining them probably starting as a work study analyst. I thought for a moment and considered the chance to move to live and work in Hove near Brighton where I had originally thought I had applied to work. Against this I quite liked Kent and Folkestone and was being well looked after at the district. The option of watching people work and using a stop watch held little attraction for me and there was also the risk of being stabbed with a pen! I was told I could consider it overnight if I wished but I had already made my decision and said I would prefer to continue training in the district. Mr Yates seemed delighted and said he thought I had made the right choice and his delight extended to ordering a tray of coffee for us and moving from behind his desk to the more friendly setting of the two armchairs in the bay window. It seemed my choice had been met favourably and we chatted for a while about which aspects of work I found most satisfying and enjoyable. I expressed an enthusiasm for maths and financial work which he seemed pleased about and then it seemed an idea was forming for him and he said that I could learn about the work that MSU was doing whilst still at the district and at the same time be making myself useful. He explained that the industrial productivity scheme was supported in the district by evaluation clerks and their work currently had a backlog due to some absences. The Productivity group was run by one manager and his assistant who also had responsibility for the clerical scheme. He knew that they would welcome some help.

The next morning I reported to their office in the same building as the engineering department and after a brief chat with them I was shown to an office across the corridor where three ladies were happily chatting across desks laden with paper forms. I was introduced as the graduate trainee, 'doing the rounds' and after I was shown what to do I would be helping them deal with the backlog. I went back to the first office and the assistant manager, Malcolm showed me the process for calculating the standard minutes that each set of tasks that were detailed on the completed job sheet covered and how the actual time taken for the task was compared to give an efficiency percentage rate. The jobs covered a variety of field tasks including replacing pole transformers, making electrical connections known as joints, to digging metres of trench and laying cables. All the components were covered by lists of tables for all the different categories on computer tabulations. The arithmetic was done using small desk calculators but I would have preferred using mental arithmetic and later found that quicker for me.

In the afternoon I joined the ladies on my own desk complete with a small mains electric calculator which I still found slower than my mental calculations but I persisted as I needed to fit in. I was shortly to find it might be difficult for me to fit in. The ladies were friendly and I discovered that the younger one was

81

very pregnant and expecting to leave in a few weeks, the other ladies were a generation older than me and I realised they were working at quite a slow pace. Between 3.30 and 4 p.m. fresh supplies of forms were brought in from the field by a number of foremen who were curious about my presence and teased my new colleagues about the growing piles of papers. The next day I wondered if I had discovered the reason for the backlog. Much of the first hour seemed to be spent drinking coffee and discussing the previous night's television with the focus mainly on episodes of Coronation Street and similar programmes that were not part of my viewing choices. There were also periods in the day when one or other of them would leave their desk and wander off somewhere else in the building, sometimes for up to half an hour. If one of their managers came in and enquired where they were then an alibi would be quickly established that they had only just left to go somewhere, perhaps to the 'Ladies.' This was sufficient to avoid any future enquiries. I wisely kept my own counsel not even enquiring whether they were meeting their own one hundred percent productivity target. I quite enjoyed the mechanics of the calculations and became more adept at touch typing the calculator although I still suspected that my mental arithmetic was quicker particularly as I wasn't distracted by retelling details of last night's tv programme's. In fact the ladies didn't really distract me and I suspected that I had been described as a temporary intruder so they were really just sitting it out. There was a distraction as the District Manager (DM) had asked the Productivity guys to help sort out a particular problem. It seemed that the field electricians who worked on repairing domestic appliances such as cookers etc did not have enough work and they had been asked to come up with some ideas and it was suggested they could employ the undoubted genius of the district's graduate trainee to help them.

We were to brainstorm it for a day and meet in the district manager's office in two days time to help fix it! I welcomed the challenge of some new creative work and in truth have a break from the storyline of the popular northern tv street. Anxious to establish my credentials I rather presumptuously declared this to be a classic mismatch of supply and demand, one of the keystones of economics. This was really stating the obvious but they seemed happy with the premise so we started to explore what could be done to reduce the supply side of the equation and what was possible to increase demand with the objective of a better match. We got down to the task with enthusiasm and came up with a number of suggestions such as redeploying some electricians onto tasks not at the vagaries of customer demands such as the periodic meter change programme, cut-out changes, public lighting maintenance and any electrical work on our own and CEGB premises. On the demand side we suggested putting out some local promotions in the press such as discounted appliance repair vouchers and encouraging more workshop repairs of smaller appliances.

All of this would be supported by predictions of programmed work and manning levels day by day and shown on coloured graphs that we had produced. On the appointed morning at 8.30 we were in the District manager's office to be met by him and his three man management team which was a little intimidating but Derek, the productivity section head outlined our proposals and I assisted with handing out the graphs. After a tense silence it was broken by the Manager who to my surprise said that he could could see the new recruit's background in economics was paying off already and instructed his three managers to put our proposal into operation and suggested that we meet again the next morning at 8 a.m. to review it. The meetings continued for a couple of weeks becoming less frequent until the monitoring and scheduling was handed over to the operational engineers but I seem to have established myself as a useful member of the district team which I was pleased about. At the same time when not producing the stats and graphs I had returned to working with the three ladies although most days one or other of them was off for some reason. A couple of a weeks into the placement there the pregnant lady left permanently and one week I was working alone in the absence of the other two. In that week I made such impressive inroads into the backlog that it was virtually up to date which I have a suspicion this progress compared with the normal output of the three regulars caused a panic to the section head who could see his productivity credentials open to some questioning. So I wasn't surprised to be moved on.

The next assignment was to complete a 'one off' annual return that was described as the Rainbow return which contrary to my initial misconception was filled in in black biro when I felt it's name called for the use of coloured crayons.

I was told that this was an industry wide annual statistical return that was returned to the Electricity council for onward transmission to the Department of Employment, I believe, to be used for unknown statistical purposes. It required examining the weekly time sheets for two sample weeks for the entire industrial workforce in the district. Values from the timesheets on allocated work, sickness other absences etc had to be extracted and entered onto the return. It looked like a massive football pools coupon, for those who have ever seen one or in recent times a spreadsheet. Large double fold out A3 sheets with multiple columns that when filled in with values needed to cross cast to sub totals and was apparently a hated task to anyone who had previously completed it. This was confirmed when during the week or so the task took if I met someone at the coffee machine or in the corridor and I answered in response to a friendly enquiry about what I was now doing, 'I am doing this year's Rainbow return.'

To be met by sympathy or barely suppressed laughter. The completion of it and the knowledge that all over the national electricity industry and possibly elsewhere in British industry a similar exercise was being completed by whichever fall guy the office could find has left me with a cynical view of any national statistics. I can see why the media often quote a nice round ten percent when they are looking for a proportion of a population say of people driving with eye problems or the proportion of nurses off sick at any point in time. Bizarrely my effort at completion was seen as a success as on some occasions the return had been 'Returned' to be resubmitted. Unbeknown to me this was something of a pyrrhic victory as the following year I was asked to complete it again when I had better things to do. I think I was older and wiser and may have copied the successful submission with minor adjustments. It saved all the effort of analysing hundreds of dusty timesheets. Maybe that explains my lack of confidence in national statistics.

The Rainbow return brought me into contact with the district accounting officer named Percy, who was to provide me with significant help in my career. He was one of three section heads reporting to the DAO, Mr Yates (despite the 1960's, the decade was still one of formality) although when we met, Percy said "call me Perce." He was responsible for the district accounting function and in this he had some fifteen people working for him. Twelve of these worked in the Trading unit which dealt with all the back office functions of invoicing etc involved in shop sales, appliance repairs and contracting wiring work etc. The other part of his responsibilities was cryptically known as MICC which wasn't some breakaway cricket club but stood for Management Information and Capital Costing. This looked pretty technical and included reporting the costs of construction and reinforcement work on the network and seemed to be the place where the engineering brethren came to make their excuses over how much money they had spent. There were also some interesting things called 'Cost investigations,'

And again this seemed to be about finding out why activities had cost more than people originally thought they would. I was told there were also some regular activities such as compiling the annual budgets for the district, monitoring actual monthly spends against the budgets and completing the end of financial years accounts.

This new, albeit temporary role was good news to my father.

At this point I should perhaps state that it had always been my father's ambition for me to become an accountant. He had worked as one but was qualified as a Chartered Company Secretary having studied for this, as he often reminded me, the hard way at night school. In fact, at university I had initially applied to a joint honours Economics and Accounting course, only switching to Joint honours in Economics and International Politics in the second year thinking it looked more interesting. So I guess I had a rudimentary grounding in some accountancy knowledge but it was really due to Percy's influence that this area of work in Seeboard started to be of interest. In any event the application of International Politics here was tangentially limited to spotting the French coast on a clear day and occasional day ferry trips to Calais or Boulogne to buy cheap wine and beer.

He made these cost investigations and budget stuff all sound interesting and was a generous and skilled teacher. I am not sure how long it was planned that I would stay in accounting but after only a few weeks events took a lucky turn, at least for me. His section head in MICC, Bob incurred an industrial injury. It sounds funny now but probably wasn't for him. One afternoon he leant back in his chair to pick up up a pen that he'd dropped and 'put his back out.' I didn't witness it as I was working across the corridor but

86

was told later that he left on a stretcher. It was quickly decided that I would occupy Bob's desk opposite Percy in the small office we now shared and over the coming weeks he gradually coached me to cover much of the work he would have done. The only difficulty was that Bob was responsible also for 'supervising' the work of two members of his staff, both ladies, a generation older than me. I had briefly spent a few days with them in the office across the corridor that they shared with the dozen people in the Trading section but other than some calculations on cost overspends and a brief introduction to something called 'reconciling monthly accounts.' The reconciling had seemed a bit mysterious and I am not sure I had understood but I was too polite to say and hoped I would either be somewhere else the next month or maybe it would make more sense the second time.

I was also concerned that the 'staff' would see me taking over and things might be uncomfortable between us but that didn't seem to happen. We got on together very well and it was suggested that as Bob's recovery was not immediate that I should assist instead in the annual budget round. It seemed that this was welcomed by the two permanent staff as they had thought they could be dragged into this process in the absence of their 'leader,' so it looked like my presence was being viewed favourably.

The reluctance to be involved they told me was based on experience as the budget round was run to a strict timetable with a number of submissions of proposed spends to Head Office who would agree them or more often, when they had totalled the sums for the whole organisation, return the proposals for reductions. At this point Percy and whoever was helping him would have to negotiate with various departments to trim their requirements and the process often became stressful with the accountant as a 'piggy in the middle,' with pressure from Head office to get the new submissions back to them. There was also talk of evening and weekend work to meet the deadlines. In fact, I found the process quite enjoyable and it introduced me to more people in the district and often the meetings felt like we were on equal footing as these managers and function heads were relying on us to get their spending plans approved by district and head office management. Percy was a diligent in ensuring that the submissions were arithmetically accurate and was patient in helping managers write the rationales for their plans, I felt I was learning a lot from this process.

In the meantime my own finances had improved to such an extent that I bought a car.

It was a gunmetal blue 1966 Triumph Herald 12/50. I was told the 12 referred to a 1200 cc engine and the

50 was the mighty 50 horse power it produced. It had a wooden dashboard, blue vinyl seats (with white piping!), a sliding vinyl sun roof, two doors, white rubber bumpers and a pair of fins at the back like a mini Cadillac. I have since discovered it was fitted with front disc brakes which I had forgotten but I do

remember it having a very tight turning circle which allowed you to do U-turns in one go in a normal road width, like London cab, (but without the non-stop, opinionated commentary!) The main advantage was I could not only see more of Kent but I could also look for a better flat and could widen my search beyond the walking distance to the office. I had found the little flat a bit gloomy in the few winter months I had spent there and although some weekends I had travelled to Kingston to see my girlfriend, other weekends had not taken me far from Folkestone town and I reckoned I had now walked around most of it more than once. The car gave me the opportunity to extend my search to include further south to Hythe and towards Romney Marsh.

Eventually I found a large ground floor flat with a garden in a detached house in Sandgate, just along the coast from Folkestone and to the south towards Hythe. It was really a suburb of Folkestone but with its own beach, shops, (mostly selling antiques,) a few

pubs and cafes and it's own little castle, part of the Napoleonic period Martello towers chain. The house was probably Victorian or even older with high ceilings and I had the entire ground floor with double fronted bay windows with sea views as well as parking on a private drive and the use of half of a large garden.

The owner, an elderly lady lived upstairs and her son came from London most weekends to shop and tend the garden. It was a great improvement on the small, dark Folkestone flat. The sea was less than a hundred yards away and pubs and take aways within walking distance. I guess the rent must have been higher than the other flat but seemed well worth it. In addition to a large kitchen and bathroom there was a long hall with some kind of glazed passage to the kitchen which seemed to be in an extension. Off the hall were two double bedrooms, a dining room and a cosy sitting room, I was living in luxury. Later that summer I married my girlfriend and the flat was our first home together.

Around the time that I took the flat I met the first people from head office that were close to my age. They were two accountants from the internal audit team, Adrian and Mark and they were full of information about the company. We managed a few evenings out together in local pubs which was good as social life, compared to university, was very limited for me apart from trips to Kingston and London. Internal Audit got a mixed welcome at the offices because their role was one of checking compliance with the Board's procedures and policies so their annual inspection was akin to an Ofsted visit to a school. Percy was very precise in what went on in accounting but I wondered whether they might unearth something that may have happened when I was in charge of engineering admin. I never heard of anything so all must have been satisfactory.

90

In the 1970's trade unionism was still predominant in Britain and this was true in the electricity industry. As part of my training I attended a couple of staff committee meetings where pressing or trivial matters were discussed between staff representatives and management. It was at such staff meetings where I learned of a phenomenon I later christened the 'canteen cat syndrome.' This occurs in large meeting groups where important items are discussed briefly particularly if they are complex and few of the attendees have anything they can sensibly contribute. At the same meeting a trivial item can be discussed for ages if no expert knowledge or previous study has been required. Such items will be the allocation of parking spaces or reallocations of office space. Such contentious topics are often loaded with emotion and indeed such was the hour and a halve's discussion on the 'Canteen Cats.' It seemed a family of stray cats had moved into the space below the Porte-a-cabin canteen at one of the depots and staff had taken to feeding them food scraps. There was a dispute between hard line folk of the pest disposal / health hazard persuasion and the soft animal lover camp. I don't remember the outcome but in later years whenever I was in a meeting which concentrated deep discussion on a matter which had little to do with matters in hand I would think of it as a 'canteen cat discussion.' Maybe I am being harsh as I never met the cats under the canteen and I am generally favourably disposed towards our feline friends. Anxious to progress my career when I was approached to stand for election as one of the office staff representatives, I readily agreed. After attending several meetings I caused a minor crisis when two of the trade union representatives cornered me to ask which white collar trade union I was a member of. Even writing those words seem like a throwback to another era, which I guess it was. My proud assertion that I thought my membership of the NUS, (The

National Union of Students,) was still current cut no
ice with the brothers.
"They are not affiliated or recognised in this industry -
you must either resign or join one of our unions." I
strongly resented this but was eventually persuaded
that I might be more of an irritant inside the tent, as
it were, so a little reluctantly, I signed up. Indeed I
think at the meetings I tried to be even handed and
balance the requirements of management with the
demands of staff but like most of the early parts of my
career it was all a learning experience. It probably
grated with me most to hear the trade unionists refer
to 'brothers' which always makes me think of monks
in a monastery.
All the time I worked in the industry in the 1970s,
even at the pinnacle of other national industrial
stoppages through strikes, I don't recall electricity
workers striking. One of my engineering colleagues
gave his explanation, transport workers and miners
can bring the country to a halt in a number of weeks -
if control room and power station staff walk out the
country is at a halt immediately, he punned, "that's
real power! "

I found the work in Accounting services interesting
and although there was much to learn Percy was a
patient and excellent tutor and I hope I was a good
pupil for him. The work was a mixture of routines and
one off investigations and enquiries and I found a
systematic elegance in the way costs of activities were
allocated into the accounting system using allocation
codes. It was interesting to investigate cost
overspends and the work brought me into contact
with all aspects of the work of the district and I was
on good terms with many of the managers and section
heads. We were generally seen as a helpful service
and the only slight friction that I remember was at the
monthly meeting with engineers to 'close off' their
capital jobs which they were often reluctant to do as it
would mean they had to give explanations for any

under or overspends from the original approved amounts. I was still working with Percy during my second winter in Folkestone and was starting to wonder whether I would soon be moved to another department so I was surprised one morning to be taken by Percy to the DAO's office, (I had become as comfortable as anyone else with the use of acronyms by now, so had clearly soaked up the culture.) The news was given to me that Bob would not be returning to work and would be taking early retirement on grounds of ill-health. As a result the job I had been doing for the past six months would need to be advertised to be filled permanently. They both said they were very happy with me in the role but I would need to consider whether I wanted to apply or whether I wanted to continue with some more experience in other departments. By way of encouragement I was told it was a grade above my current one so there would be a salary increase and also that Personnel at head office did not have a problem with me ceasing training and taking up a permanent position. I felt I was being given some helpful hints and said I would think about it but would give my answer first thing the next day. I think I had already decided that I would apply for the position and Percy was very keen that I should. He also said that the senior of the two ladies in the section had already said she hoped I would stay in the role and held no personal ambitions herself. Betty was a self contained Scottish lady who some staff found aloof but we seemed to get along well. Quite early on I had admitted to her that I didn't fully understand some of her accounting duties and they looked very complex. I was serious and she seemed to appreciate it so she patiently explained it to me again and 'supervised' me one month while I did the account reconciliations and announced that she could now take her holidays more freely as she hadn't let Bob deal with them in her absence as he had once messed them up. I must admit I hoped I still remembered what to do by the time her holiday occurred.

I had been warned that there would be other applications for the MICC position both from within the district and possibly from neighbouring districts. My appointment was certainly not a foregone conclusion and apparently in such appointments an independent manager from head office would sit on the interview panel. This was also described as a way of assessing future talent that may have a later career at head office. All of this did nothing to calm any nerves and although memories of the interview itself is long lost to me I do remember being nervous and later very relieved when I was appointed. Percy was so pleased he took me out for a pub lunch and said that he hadn't looked forward to helping settle in a new assistant and he was pleased that things could go on as before, which suited me too. The salary increase was welcome as although the flat was comfortable we were saving a deposit to buy our own first house and any increase in annual salary would help with the mortgage loan calculation.

That autumn, newly married, we bought our first house, a terraced Victorian house within walking distance of the office and near a nice park with a few local shops nearby.

It was enjoyable working with Percy but I discovered his dedication to work was legendary. He live some way up the east Kent coast but apparently always made it into work, even through the Kent winter weather which could bring blizzards and snow drifts. There was some story I was told that he had even driven himself to work when he had a leg in plaster, operating one pedal with a walking stick! I found this story hard to believe but my opinion was revised when one day he arrived into the office mid-morning, having warned me he would be late in. He looked pale and tight lipped carrying a bloodied handkerchief in

94

one hand and said "I've been to the dentist and had all my teeth out to have false teeth."
In fact he actually said "aaggived ogg ddenggissgts ggttnn ggyy grrdeedd ggatken gout " or something like it. These were gents who had seen wartime service as teenagers, so were made of strong stuff!

Somewhere about this time I had started a correspondence course to qualify as an accountant having discovered that my BSc Econ gave me partial exemptions in some two out of five parts of the exams.

Leaving Folkestone for Sutton

I left Kent reluctantly as there was an option hinted to me that if I stayed in Folkestone there was a likelihood of Percy retiring within twelve months but in the meantime the same position in Croydon became vacant and I applied for the job. I was interviewed and although it seemed to go well the job went to someone already carrying out the role in the smaller neighbouring district of Sutton. The Croydon job would have been a promotion of two grades while Sutton was a promotion of one. It was suggested to me that an application from me for the Sutton job was anticipated so I applied despite never having visited the London Borough of Sutton before unless I had unknowingly driven through it. The offices were in the centre of town in a 1930's building above a large Seeboard shop.

The interview panel was their DAO, a large man, and their District manager a man half his size who I had heard was the board's first district manager who wasn't an engineer and consequently something of a legend in his own lunchtime. I was pleased to see that the third panel member was the same head office accountant who interviewed me at Croydon as well as for the MICC job in Kent and I felt it was nice to see a friendly face. I believe I answered all the technical questions well but was slightly thrown by the manager asking whether it would be a problem for me to be the supervisor of the dozen or so staff most of whom would be older than me. I sensed some tension in the panel when the head office accountant pointed out that the previous incumbent had been appointed at the same age and had now been promoted. I wisely thought it best to stay out of the ensuing argument but sensed that there was some resentment amongst the district management and the head office representative and I learned later that this was definitely the case. In the event I was offered the job and we now needed to sell the house in Folkestone and find somewhere to live in Surrey.

Initially, in the week I stayed in a small hotel in Sutton, returning to Folkestone most weekends but also spending some weekends with my wife viewing houses in Surrey. We eventually found a house on a leafy modern estate. It was a change from our Victorian house in Folkestone and benefitted from central heating and a small garden. It was off Reigate Hill and a ten mile drive south from the office and it felt as near as we wanted to be to outer London.

 Atmosphere in the office was more 'edgy' if that's the right word and it made me realise that the Folkestone office was a much more benign environment. In the new office the DAO and the DM did not seem to enjoy a good relationship and any errors or customer complaints led to inquests over who the culprit was to be told off.
The DAO resented the fact that the DM was an Admin Officer from another district who had previously been an equal but now was promoted to be his boss. The term boss was accurate for both of them. The senior of them enjoyed the imperial sounding Christian name of Augustus and his imperiousness lived up to

97

it. Another characteristic particularly of the DAO was a great enthusiasm in finding fault with anything that came out of Head Office or the Computer Centre. Documents were distributed first thing in the morning from boxes delivered by overnight couriers and nothing pleased him more than being the first district to phone in a correction, however minor, to Head Office and ideally get someone into trouble.

I could see that if I had any future career ambitions in either of those directions I would need to balance my position locally with how I might be viewed from Head office. A couple of months after my appointment there was a pleasant development when the board decided that all the accounting heads in the districts merited the same grade as the responsibilities were equal so I received a welcome upgrade. When it was announced I received a phone call from my predecessor who realised he had made an unnecessary move to Croydon for an upgrade and could have stayed and benefitted without moving.

I sympathised but was happy with the outcome to my advantage.

I was fortunate in the accounting position too have a section full of of pleasant competent people, it may have lulled me into a false sense of security over the difficulties of managing staff. The management information team were headed by Mike who was younger than me by a couple of years and had only been appointed to the role a couple of months previously. We became good friends, having lunch together and meeting socially and as I had only just been promoted from the same role in Kent I was able to guide him in any areas that he needed but he was very energetic, ambitious and a quick learner which meant he was keen to cover for me when I took any holidays. My other section head, Cliff, was much older and had served in the merchant navy in the war on the Russian convoys so I am sure any customer complaints or tantrums from the district management were met by him with the weight they deserved. He

98

knew his job inside out and I mostly let him and his staff get on with things, he generally came to tell me about things he has already done and the only interventions I remember were standing between him and the frequently agitated shop manger from downstairs who like to complain loudly about some trivial paperwork matter that he felt the trading section staff had let him down on. Cliff calmly stood there while the manager ranted some inches below him and I usually ushered the manager out saying he could put his complaint in writing if he felt like it while really fearing that Cliff might one day lose it and throw him down the stairs which given the size disparity seemed a distinct possibility.

 At some stage while at Sutton I must have lost my temper and had some kind of public vocal outburst; given that this must have been some five or six years since I started work at Seeboard it was obviously a rare event and I think most people would have described me as affable and easy going. Whatever the event was, and I don't remember, although it was probably either the shop manager or a hard of thinking engineer, it was relayed back to me some years later when I arrived in new office, managing a large number of staff. One of them told me that some urban myth preceded me and that he had heard that my outward cheery exterior masked a fearsome temper that once seen was never forgotten. I remember that I had to suppress my amusement and mutter "well it's a rare thing, thankfully," before retreating to my office where I could chuckle in peace. I don't think I ever lost my temper there but it was a useful facet of my secret personality to have in reserve.There was one other minor staff difficulty and that was with one of the trading section ladies who had a punctuality problem and would arrive in the office ten minutes or so late on many occasions. Like Reggie Perrin in the TV series she would breathlessly describe elaborate scenarios of lorries shedding their loads or trees blocking roads despite the fact that many of the other staff took similar routes and were in on time. Her shortened hours caused resentment among the others so for a week or so I recorded and totalled the missing minutes and presented her with the option of working at the end of the day to make it up or working through one lunch hour. Her reply of not being able to get her shopping done I met with stoney silence and raised eyebrows from me but it cured the issue for a while and had the benefit of raising my popularity among the other staff.The job was interesting, I managed the district's accounts, prepared and monitored the capital and revenue budgets. Maintained good contacts with a number of head office departments. I don't recall any real difficulties with the annual internal audit reports so it seemed that I had got the hang of the role and as often happened in my career a new opportunity presented itself.

It was proposed, as a career development, that the Income head at   the district should swap jobs with me so for six months I would head up the district customer accounting function. In the new temporary role I managed many more staff, over a hundred in total, including the field industrial staff of meter readers, collectors and disconnection staff. The three office departments I was to manage were debt collection, (which I had worked in early in my career,) customer records of which I had very little knowledge and meter reading which again I knew little about. It became an object lesson to me in being effective without necessarily being an expert. The person who was the permanent head of Income was experienced, much older than me and very well respected so the staff were used to bringing their problems to him to solve and expected to do the same with me. I quickly learned that asking the right questions and working with them to come up with solutions was the only way to do this and the staff learned that I was less agitated about the problems, even when it appeared that mistakes had been made, than my predecessor and there were a number of reasons for this.

Firstly there was probably my naivety, often I didn't initially understand the problem so would calmly ask a series of questions and rarely get too excited.

Secondly, I would never criticise the member of staff publicly but would check that they would learn from what had happened and look together to avoid future instances through training or cross checks.

Finally, much of the drama was caused by the reaction to errors by the DAO or DM and the fear of them finding out a mistake or an error was so strong that whole catalogues of complaints or errors had been previously admitted to them -'in case they subsequently found out,' when the criticism was even more severe.

My tactic was to only reveal some of the mistakes after they had been sorted out or if I thought the press or consumers council were aware or likely to become so. Otherwise we would sort things if we could without exposure up the line. If there was a later exposure I would take the criticism with replies such as "I didn't think you should be involved in such as trivial matter when you have the whole district to run and I have resolved it - I thought that was what I am paid for."

I believe it helped that I wasn't afraid of either of these two bullies, one of whom I had difficulty taking seriously as he would get very agitated and red in the face and looked in danger of an imminent coronary event. The other was small and if issuing rebukes would stand up and raise himself off his heels but still could only glare at me from some four or five inches below. My confidence was helped in two other ways; one was the realisation my working with them would be a temporary matter as I was already aiming to move to a more influential role perhaps in head office. The other was when the DM brought his wife along to an evening social event and when he introduced me to her as one of his senior staff her reply of "You seem very young for this position- I hope you don't let my

101

little Gussie bully you!" His suppressed rage was a picture and although I don't recall my reply as I was trying very hard not to laugh out loud, he didn't ever try to bully me again.

Working in the Income department definitely gave me some new experiences, valuable in retrospect but some of them unsettling at the time. I was now experienced in dealing with customers on the phone and in some cases face to face in the office when people with outstanding bills were pleading for more time to pay and my staff needed to escalate the negotiations. What I hadn't done was to accompany one of the disconnection staff to take the final step so one day I offered to put this right. In the morning we visited a few domestic customers, most paid on the doorstep in full, a couple offered post dated cheques and several were actually disconnected by the electrician removing the customer's main fuse. In the afternoon we visited a few commercial customers, mostly small industrial units who handed over cheques but things got more interesting in Sutton High Street. The first shop after keeping us waiting found someone authorised to sign the cheque after Bill, the electrician had shown we meant business by opening the switch cabinet near the door and took his tools out to start to remove the fuses. Suddenly the shop assistant went from "I don't think any authorised signatory is on the premises," to a more concerned "Just give me five minutes - I'll be back with payment."

Our reception at the local branch of the electrical store, Dixons, was met with disbelief. A haughty shop manager said he knew nothing about a two month's overdue account of several hundreds of pounds and we would have to speak to their accounts office. I pointed out the accounts, reminders and disconnection notice were all addressed to this shop and perhaps he better speak to his accounts office but if nothing was arranged by way of payment we would be leaving with the main fuses. He went away to phone them and returned to confidently tell us that his head office had said we couldn't do that. With some pleasure I told him that we were legally entitled to do that and I walked with Bill to the back of the shop where our records had told us we would find the switch board and fuses. What we hadn't realised, or maybe just me, was pulling the fuses and plunging a shop lit by banks of tv's and shelf lighting, with the only light coming in from the shop front some fifty yards away which was partially covered with posters and the window display did not make for an easy exit. The more experienced Bill came to the rescue with a torch from his bulky tool bag and we made our escape with the shop manager shouting after us rather feebly, "you can't do this - YOU CAN'T!" Despite clear evidence to the contrary. I was pleased to meet with him in our shop below the office when he arrived the next day with the cheque that had been couriered to him from their head office. I resisted the urge to tell him that the Seeboard shop had had a busy afternoon with customers who had been surprised to find our competitor closed - I felt that might be rubbing salt in the wound.

The promotion to the Sutton job gave us an improved standard of living which included holidays abroad and the addition of a second family car - a real cliche in that it was a bright red convertible sports car.

Looking back I feel that working in the Sutton office was one of the less happy experiences of my life. Whether it was the responsibility at an early age although no one suggested that I couldn't do either of the two jobs I had there. It may have been the general atmosphere in the office; there were definite fears that the district was in danger of amalgamation with either of it's two larger neighbours. The management style was unhelpful there with scapegoating from the two layers of management above me and there was a constant need to protect my staff from them. Certainly life in the Kent office had been more measured and friendlier and I believe the office was run just as effectively, if not more so. Perhaps it was the outer London city location, certainly I felt less oppressed once I had driven south to the leafier environs off Reigate hill. I had also been talked into continuing my part-time studies in accountancy which entailed evening classes in Kingston on Thames after work on two nights a week and never really found this to my liking.

Horsley towers

In those days many organisations were enthusiastic about training courses and often ran their own training establishments. As well as attendance at Seeboard's own staff college there was also a national industry training centre in Surrey known at Horsley Towers, owned and run by the Electricity Council, the industry umbrella body. Architecturally this was even more impressive than North Frith as can be seen by the photo here, having been designed by the architect of the Houses of Parliament, Sir Charles Barry, in a regency gothic style. In the present day it's run as a hotel and wedding venue.

My first attendance there was for a communications and presentations course and although the main building and public rooms were impressive, including a large gothic chapel, accommodation was more rudimentary in wooden outbuildings with communal washrooms. The course was helpful with video recording of presentations followed by criticism. My own particular stumbling block was a tendency to pause in my presentation and punctuate the speech with an 'Umm' before continuing. The tutor had a harsh remedy by getting the rest of the class to count the 'Umms' on their fingers which after two repeats completely cured me. He suggested clamping my jaw and going for a dramatic pause whenever I felt like 'Umming,' I think someone had given the ex-PM Gordon Brown the same advice which may have explained his pausing and jaw jutting during speeches. All in all it was a valuable couple of days and I gained greater confidence in speaking and presenting which I would find useful throughout my career.

Computing in Worthing

My leaving Sutton district was initially temporary. Unbeknown to me the company was planning a large scale reorganisation and part of this was the amalgamation of some districts and the subsequent closure of some offices. There had always been rumours that the smaller district offices were under threat and it was obvious that this was a way to reduce some costs through rationalisation. At the time secondments were extensively used in the organisation, possibly as a way of giving people wider experience whilst reducing the risk of making a permanent appointment to someone later found to be unsuitable. But at a time of change it also gave greater flexibility in the staffing with fewer staff in permanent positions and grades. After my secondment to the Executive Officer Income post, effectively a job swap with the Income EO taking my job in Accounting, I had applied for a secondment promotion to the assistant DAO position in the next and larger district of Kingston on Thames. At the same time I expressed an interest in a secondment to train as a systems analyst at the data centre in Worthing. I didn't seem to hit it off with the district manager at Kingston and I felt the head office representative knew about my other application. In any event the Kingston secondment went to John, a colleague at Sutton who was older and more experienced than me and the following week I was interviewed for the systems analyst secondment at Worthing which was offered to me. The fact it was a secondment made it easier for me as I could say goodbye to my colleagues and explain that I would be back, although I knew this was by no means a certainty.

The plan was that at the end of the 1970's Seeboard was rapidly embracing more modern business methods and a major initiative was to use its large,

106

expensive and allegedly powerful main frame computer to automate a number of business processes. To help do this the theory was that some users could be brought in from the sharper end of the operation to assist in these developments. I joined the System's planning section along with three other 'user secondees' in the early summer of 1980 some four years after I had joined the Sutton office. The four of us Bill, Jeff, Paul and myself had different backgrounds and were to provide 'user expertise' from the operational end of the business. The training programme was strange and a mixture of spending time between the development teams we would be working with and weeks of American (I think from IBM,) audio visual training aids, so much so we joked between ourselves in mock American accents, well you have to take your fun where you can get it. We were a bit of a novelty to the permanent staff there, most of whom were close to my age and were either trained as computer programmers or operators. I got off to an inauspicious start by driving fast down from my home in Reigate and not observing the speed limit in the company car park. Apparently this was observed by an angry administration manager from his office on the top floor who spent part of the day searching out the unfamiliar maniac in a red, open topped sports car. When we met, his public complaining to me about it won me a number of new friends in the building. His pathological obsession of all things relating to safety and matters of the car park had made him the least popular man in the building and my irritation of him was to be celebrated. Despite our different career paths we were welcomed into the department. Some of the older and more senior members of staff had been recruited over ten years earlier from districts of the regional pre-computer billing centres.

The younger programmers and analysts were less knowledgable about the districts and the users and we felt there was an opportunity for us all to develop

107

better mutual understandings particularly if the new systems being developed were to be effective.

The working environment was different to the district offices; for a start there were far fewer incoming phone calls and to some extent it made for a quieter more academic environment. Programmers and analysts would sit quietly studying their coding input sheets or the tabulated output sheets. When I joined, monitors like pc screens, had only been introduced into the computer hall itself and application programmes were tested by typing into a keyboard in the keying room which would send the instructions to the mainframe and print a reference copy onto paper or in some cases produce a pack of punched cards that had to be taken into the computer hall. Then a programmer would have waited their turn at the limited number of keyboards and then return to their office to await the output to be printed out from the printers in the computer hall. They would collect those and examine it back at their desks for errors or expected results. The gaps between input and output was often spent chatting in other offices with colleagues, it made the atmosphere there very sociable and combined with the on-site staff restaurant and social club and bar made it a relatively relaxed place to work. There was also a playing field, squash ladder to join with games in a nearby sports centre

It made it the most sociable environment I had worked in since university some eight years before.

The atmosphere and the somewhat eccentric character of some of the fellow inmates gave rise to a few amusing instances that I recall during my time there.

Television series such as the 'IT Crowd' and 'The Big Bang Theory,' have capitalised on the otherworldliness and OCD nature of some folk that are drawn to the world of IT and computer programming and the department had more than its fair share of characters. I remember one relatively new programmer who despite wearing some kind of crumbled suit, with a mass of hair, like a halo around his head and chin, resembled some kind of hobbit. His look was complemented by a flapping sound as he walked down the corridor which was traced after a few days to the soles of his shoes which through wear were semi-detached from the uppers. When this was pointed out to him he answered that he had wondered why his socks were getting wet! His manager advised replacement footwear on the grounds of health and safety.

Another young programmer was a skinhead with the hairstyle complemented by Doc Martin boots, high hitched trousers and braces. He was known as 'John effing,' on account of his colourful use of adjectives and was something of a practical joker and through this had some kind of feud going on with another member of the department. His adversary thought he had the chance to get even when he noticed a pair of braces trailing below the closed cubicle door in the gents toilets. Seizing the opportunity to get even, the braces were given a hard yank, provoking a crashing sound from within the cubicle where it sounded as if the occupant had suddenly been catapulted from their throne. The culprit exited the scene only to see John effing walking towards him carrying a pile of prints from the computer hall and still wearing his distinctive braces. Minutes later the red-faced and angry Assistant Chief accountant who ran the department was stalking the corridor looking intently at anyone for signs of undisguised mirth. We all looked innocent as the incident had not yet been broadcast to us until the culprit was back at his desk and heard to say quietly - "I didn't know the boss wore braces -I've never seen him take his suit jacket off!"

I was unknowingly the instigator of a mystery incident in the building. It was a wintery day and Worthing had experienced a snowfall the previous evening and through the night. Anticipating possibly having to push my car or even abandon it and walk, I had found a stout pair of boots that looked like the best footwear for the next day. Unfortunately, their bright yellow / tan colour would clash dreadfully with my grey or blue suits and being more conscious of my appearance than some of my colleagues I used some black shoe dye that evening on them and left it to dry overnight. The next day I drove to the office and sloshed through the snow and slush in the car park but my feet inside my newly blackened boots were warm and dry. Sitting next to the radiator to ensure that they outsides dried off I gradually became aware of a strong chemical smell. I walked down the corridor to the admin office for some stationary supplies and noticed the smell was in that office too. I took a detour to the coffee machine where there was already a small gathering of people some of whom were discussing the strange chemical smell. The consensus was that the Beecham's pharmaceuticals factory next door must be emitting some new odours and one colleague was off to see our facilities manager to ask whether it was our own air con plant or Beecham's and if it was them would they do something about it as it was surely noxious and unhealthy.

All morning whichever part of the building I went to the smell was there. It was only at lunchtime when I was in my small two seater car and the smell nearly knocked me out when the heater had warmed up on the drive to the bank in town that something registered. It was my boot dye that was smelling so pungent and any heat had made it worse. I drove home and changed my footwear and back at the office agreed with my colleagues that the smell was gradually improving. I didn't hear whether Beechams had been accused and I didn't ever admit my guilt or wear those boots to the office again.

It was some weeks before we finished the course of tutorials not all of which would be relevant to our

110

projects but it did give us a good theoretical grounding in systems analysis and a broad view of modern computing. The projects we were to work on were all designed to take on-line data transactions out to the districts to allow updates to files through what were called VDT's (yes back to the old acronyms again - visual display terminals.) Essentially keyboards and on-line computer screens, with the actual processing still competed on the mainframe in Worthing but replacing the sending of paper forms and outputs. I had been originally recruited to work on on-line expenditure accounting which I had good knowledge and experience of. Life never works out that way as quite early on the manager of the data centre, a rather aloof figure, summoned me to his large office. Here he explained that priorities had changed and development of an on-line expenditure system had been deferred but there was going to be a development of an on-line payroll system for industrial staff and did I have a good knowledge of this. I felt I was being put on the spot here but had spent all of two weeks in a district payroll section some five years before but rashly concluded this was probably more than anyone else in the building and I was reluctant for the secondment to end so gave him a confident "Yes, I know my way around the payroll system."
I was keen to continue the secondment for a number if reasons. First and foremost I was enjoying the opportunity to learn new skills in a new environment. I liked the district work but positions at my level came with responsibilities for staff. In the Sutton Income position I was notionally responsible for over a hundred people when including the industrial staff of meter readers, collectors and disconnectors. Relinquishing these responsibilities, even temporarily was quite liberating. I also realised that the four of us recently drafted in from district had more relevant knowledge of operations and the confidence of youth coupled with a desire to continue the secondment persuaded me to agree the change of project.

Although we were spending most of our time in the initial few months in the training room the four of us were already assigned to teams of programmers and analysts who we would work on the project with and offices we would have our desks in. I was now assigned to the Personnel and Payroll development team were a friendly and helpful group of people. Two of them had worked in the organisation before the data centre was established and two had only worked in the data centre. The project was ok but payroll wasn't a particular interest of mine but I guess the learning experience from this was seeing how computer systems are planned, developed, tested and introduced. The other benefit was gaining personal contacts at the computer centre and these were to prove very valuable in the following years.

While at Worthing my first marriage ended after seven years so I needed to move house and being on secondment added to the uncertainty. At the time I received some helpful advice from the Deputy Chief Accountant who had originally appointed me on the secondment. He became something of a mentor and was instrumental later to arrange my appointment to head office when I was feeling a bit stranded after my district was merged and my old office closed. As someone who had also experienced a divorce he advised it was more important to sort out your personal life as a priority and this would allow you to sort your career out later. This was good advice as later that year a new girlfriend and myself got together and bought a house in Worthing, we are still together forty years later and it was the best thing that ever happened to me.

The house was in a western suburb of the town near local shops with a railway station and a number of pubs. The house was exactly a hundred years old and named Snow Cottage, we were told because the winter of 1880 had been a severe one and heavy

112

snow falls had interrupted the completion of building it.

Head Office

My secondment had been extended to over twelve months and due to some arrangement with the Inland Revenue I had to notionally leave the Worthing office for a week and relocate for one week to another office nearer home. I didn't really understand the logic of this but was told that the secondment could recommence as a new one a week later and if this break wasn't arranged then any travelling and subsistence payments made to me in the first twelve months would be liable to a tax demand. Sensing a financial penalty as the expenses had been generous and very welcome I agreed and spent a week in the payroll section in Guildford. I was welcomed here as one of the ex-district IT gurus who were devising the new whizz bang computerised payroll system although I was aware that it was likely to put some of the staff out of a job. I put those concerns to one side as the organisation at that time was reasonably benevolent and were operating a 'no redundancy' policy using early retirements and redeployments for displaced staff. The next week I returned to the system planning section having greatly increased my minimal hands on experience at the sharp end of payroll and having kept my expenses out of the hands of the taxman.

During this time we moved house from Reigate to Worthing buying an eccentric flint detached cottage in the village of Tarring, a western suburb of Worthing. That is a whole story in itself as it was previously run as a dog parlour by a lady who proudly stated she hadn't cut anything down in the large walled garden during the seven years she had lived there; and it showed! There were also several rooms full of dolls and teddy bears 'rescued' from local charity shops. We moved ourselves and put all the furniture in the large garage while we sanded floorboards and paintwork and tried to get rid of the clinging' damp dog' aroma. It was our first home together for us and our dog, Stan, a rescued greyhound wolfhound cross, and we all loved it. The first years in Snow Cottage was a busy time; the energy of youth allowed us both to do a full day's work, walk the dog before and after work and spend many evenings renovating and decorating the cottage. We were ambitious, ripping out ceilings, plumbing, replacing fireplaces as well as decorating and restoring the cottage garden. Eventually we commissioned a friend who had newly qualified as an architect to design and project manage a large extension on the back of the cottage and Kelvin did us proud with this.

There is a link here to contemporary photos
https://snowcottage.home.blog/

All this activity went on while we both worked hard at our careers with my move to a position at head office seeing me taking a more pressurised role than I had enjoyed in computer planning.

When I took up a position in head office I imagined that it would be in the grand seafront Victorian building on Hove seafront but at that time the old building was undergoing an extensive renovation and having a new wing built on the side. Temporarily some head office functions were sharing space with the Sussex district office slightly further to the west along the coast in Portslade. I had been told by the deputy chief Accountant, Bob that there would be good career prospects for me in the Chief Accountants department even going so far as to say it may not be necessary for me to recommence my accountancy studies which I had already abandoned. It was suggested that my experience in district coupled with my recent time developing computer systems would give me some unique advantages to developing policies at head office, particularly relating to customer accounting which was the responsibility of the Income section. Not mentioned by Bob was how the head of Income would feel about my appointment without him having the chance to interview or even meet me.

This was a little unsettling as I knew this manager, Harry, only by reputation of being strong minded, 'not suffering fools,' but well respected. Before I left Worthing a colleague there gave me some comforting advice along the lines of "he doesn't get along with a lot of people, he often takes against them but I think you will be fine with him once he gets used to the idea."

The first day in the new job didn't bode well as Harry met me, shook hands and said he was going to Croydon, one of the district offices, all day and would be back tomorrow, and left. The other member of his staff, Tom was friendly and showed me to the coffee machine and staff restaurant and said Harry would be pleased if we handled any queries by phone or memo that day as he was deep into writing some new procedures for the districts to follow and would probably not speak to us for a few days! Later that day after answering a few queries from district which went well as a number if them were from people I knew and they were pleasantly surprised to find me in head office and exchanged the usual jokey prejudices of my having to become less practical if I was on head office staff.

While Harry was away there was a call from the Chief Accountant's secretary asking me to go and see him so entering his large office expecting a welcome I was given a customer's complaint letter that had apparently come to him from the Chairman. "Where's Harry? - he usually deals with these, it got to the chairman and he wants it replied to today! Are you the new bod that Bob has found?" No more pleasantries were exchanged and I left asking whether he wanted to see the reply -"No thanks sent it out and copy in the chairman and make sure he will be satisfied with the answer."

I felt it was something of a baptism of fire but realised that I wasn't worried what the chairman thought but more worried about Harry but after sitting at my desk with a cup of coffee concluded this was no different from the hundreds of letters I had written answering customer complaints in my career and we had dealt with occasional letters that had come to us via the chairman's office. I don't remember the actual details now but I contacted the district office to get background details and composed the reply, got it typed (yes - back in the day secretaries and typists produced the letters!)

After I talked it over with Tom we sent it off with a copy to the chairman - then hid under my desk -(not really but I did feel it was some sort of trial.)

Harry came in after me the next morning and said he was going off to a quiet conference room to work on his new procedure and the accompanying board paper to get approval and would Tom and me deal with the phones and the post and not bother him. He asked if all was quiet yesterday and I said there wasn't anything we hadn't been able to deal with but he needed to know there had been a letter to the chairman that the chief accountant had asked me to reply that day. Harry got excited - "what was the letter about, where was the reply, was the chief happy with it, what did the chairman say, had I checked with district ?" I handed the letter and my reply to him and he quietly read them and I could see he was about to say something then stopped -

 "I'll be in the meeting room - Tom knows where if the chairman calls then interrupt me -otherwise I'll see you tomorrow."

I felt I had passed some kind of test but was relieved that we heard nothing more about that particular complaint and Harry didn't ever ask to see any of my replies to complaint letters unless I specifically asked his advice.

A week or so later Harry finished his procedure writing and passed out his board paper for approval and as a result a sea change came over him. He talked to me about the projects that he anticipated we would need to initiate and asked me about my time in district and how I had got on with the system planning staff. He also asked for my personal assessments of individuals and although I tried to be reasonably diplomatic with my replies he certainly didn't hold back on his assessments. I was somewhat reassured by a certain alignment of opinion of those people that I had first hand knowledge of and I was pleased that he described the deputy as someone he had a lot of time for and admitted he had only been willing to accept me into the section on Bob's personal assurances that it would work out well for us both.

I must admit in my career I would be very wary about someone recruiting an assistant for me so I was pleased that things seemed to be working out ok for us.

In fact all the time we worked together I don't remember a serious disagreement between us and I believe I learned a lot from Harry about managing people and to focus on the end result; allowing people to use their own preferred approaches to get there rather than being prescriptive on how they should achieve the results. I also think I learned from him how to look at business processes and improve them and to question whether things were being done in the most effective way. His visits to district to canvas those who's opinion he valued were also instructive. Here he would take a DAO or an Income manager into his confidence and say to them that he was considering making some changes to a particular business process and it might look a bit like this and what did they think, would it work, what would they need to make it succeed. In this way he built support at an early stage and could genuinely say to the board we have taken soundings with operational people and they are supportive. It was different to some of my previous experiences with some of the expenditure systems that appeared to have been launched untested and without user support.

118

There were occasions when Tom or myself were despatched by Harry to one of the districts to 'float' one of the new ideas and gauge reaction and we would often speculate whether the idea was privately thought to outlandish for Harry to personally launch but a kinder view is that he was just developing our skills

I also learnt during this time that it was important to keep questioning how things were done and that it was important to keep looking at ways to improve business practices. As a utility providing an essential service it was also important to ensure we didn't introduce things into our systems that put customers at a disadvantage particularly those in vulnerable groups either through health or finances. This had to be balanced with ensuring that we maintained the financial viability of the organisation that is we collected monies owed to us. The rights of customers were also scrutinised by our consumer regulatory body, both regional and nationally and there was always press coverage to consider who were always keen to represent the 'poor little customer' against the big, bad electricity board. It was definitely a balancing act but the creativity, attention to detail and diplomacy required made the process all the more interesting and I really felt my abilities and skills were being employed and developed more in this role than any previous one.

Tom was a helpful and cheerful colleague and knew his way around the large head office and how to deal with queries from the consumer council, the press and other departments. I look back on this time as a particularly happy one both in work and at home having got remarried and enjoyed the social life afforded on the busy south coast with visiting friends and the cultural opportunities afforded by Brighton. This role in the income section felt for the first time that I was doing something creative and it was important to get right as the things we were doing impinged in a small way on many people's lives. In some way we seemed different in our outlook to many of our colleagues in head office and maybe this was because some of the functions were more inward looking meeting the internal needs of the organisation. This wasn't true of every head office department and as well as keeping in touch with the district staff who were operating the procedures and policies we were developing there were others. These included the commercial engineers in the tariffs department who were responsive for setting customers prices and together with us would develop the communications with customers on the bills and reminders etc.

Another group we worked closely with were the metering engineers who had responsibility for sourcing supplies of meters and ensuring those on circuit were certified. Their main meter test station was in a grand house in its own grounds below Box Hill in Surrey. Seeboard seemed to have accumulated a number if these type of buildings, in some cases inheriting them at nationalisation from the previous municipal and rural electricity undertakings. A similar one was outside East Grinstead and housed our engineering control centre along with a co-located CEGB facility. Allegedly because if the strategic importance of these facilities they did not appear on any published maps apart from our own!

One memorable demonstration I remember at the metering station was the refurbishment of the cases in glass tanks where they were cleaned by high pressure airstreams containing crushed nut shells. It was not the only time in my career that I shared a room with a load of nuts!

The role was very outward looking in comparison with some other head office positions as it was necessary to be closely in touch with both the district staff operating the customer policies and the computer planning department as more and more computerisation of the business processes were being applied. I realised the value of my previous

120

experience both in the districts and the computer planning department gave me an almost unique perspective as well as useful personal contacts which go a long way in business to help things along. I spent a fair proportion of those couple of years travelling out to our offices across the south east of England. With offices in the far flung corners of Kent in Hythe, Broadstairs and Rochester being quite a drive from home in Worthing it made for some long working days but it was important to maintain the dialogues and I don't think I was ever accused of being one of those remote people in the ivory towers of head office. It wasn't all plain sailing as there was pressure on all sorts of customer metrics such as debt write offs, outstanding accounts, meter fraud, meter reading access and other measures of performance. When new policies were being developed I often found it was good practice to allow the most cynical or vocal opponent of the change to run a pilot trial and even though there was often criticism and friction it could be the best way to debug the process.

The other advantage with the driving to districts was that as my role wasn't considered operational enough for a company car I was paid what was described as a casual users mileage rate which covered fuel costs but also was a generous contribution towards other motoring costs. When I was first transferred to head office I was bizarrely driving a huge Jaguar XJ6 which we had bought in a fit of madness, exchanging my girlfriends almost new Fiat for this five year old luxurious monster. I used it several times to visit districts often taking the precaution of parking in the far corner of the car park wherever possible. My cover was blown when the assistant chief accountant Chris, who was mine and Harry's manager, announced one cold winter's morning that we would travel to Rochester office together for a meeting and would I mind driving as his company car, a base model Ford Escort popular was reluctant to start in the cold. When we arrived in the road outside at my green XJ6 he was shocked,

"I've seen this about - I thought it was the chairman's."

'No, his is dark green and slightly newer. This is mine and we paid for it, unlike him,' I replied, helpfully.

I could see he wasn't happy, so I told him I usually parked it out of sight of any windows when visiting districts which I am not sure he believed but I hoped to sow the seeds of my campaign to be entitled to a company car.

I had an interesting working relationship with Chris that I suspect amused both of us. One of his characteristics was writing and rewriting other peoples memos and letters. As if this wasn't bad enough it was his method for doing it that was so painful. His secretary would call you into his large seafront office where you would trawl through every word of the document, dictating and redrafting it to one of the long suffering secretaries. Then while she would go off to type it he would take the opportunity to discuss some current policy or issue of the day. I didn't dislike working for him but found these pedantic sessions a waste of my time when I could be doing something more useful and believed my written English was every bit as good as his and often told him so. His answer was usually something along the lines of him being keen to ensure consistent policy messages emanating from the department, or some other management speak woffle.

I am not sure whether I actually set a deliberate trap or whether it arose from a happy combination of circumstances. It went something like this.

His secretary brought me a customer complaint letter that had arrived via the chairman's office with specific request the reply was made promptly, it may have come from an MP and it related to some policy which I have long forgotten the details of.

Chris was an assistant chief accountant with responsibilities among others for customer policies but

122

was out of the office that day. I researched the issue, spoke to the district concerned, drafted a reply and took it to Peter, the chief accountant, who quickly read it, said it was fine and signed it on behalf of the chairman and it was posted out that night.

The next day I was called into Chris's office where he held up a copy of the original letter to the chairman and explained we would draft a response. I started to say that there was no need but he held up his hand and said forcefully,

"We have talked about this before and I know you believe it is a waste of your time." To which I replied that he was right. Undaunted he called in his secretary and we spent the next hour painfully constructing a reply to what was something of a complex issue. The typed draft was brought in and we both had a copy each and some more rewrites were done. Eventually, the final copy was brought and he said he would take it to the Chief accountant for signature and to his surprise I told him he had no need to do that. I then explained that a signed response had gone the previous day - "Why didn't you tell me!" he spluttered and after I replied that he wouldn't let me and we should both use it as a learning experience. I made a quick exit to go back to the office and share my amusement and triumph with Tom. Interestingly, our joint letter and memo composition sessions became much rarer events after this.

Views on helping customers with difficulties in payment had to be sought and agreed with the consumers consultative committee who independently represented their rights. As their regional office was in Royal Tunbridge Wells and there was a sprinkling of military and other titles as well as some double barrelled surnames amongst their members I leave you to imagine their composition. They had an important and necessary role to perform and in any industry it certainly pays to have the regulatory body at least in dialogue with the possibility of gaining agreement to your proposals. Early on I was able to engender some credibility with them by calling on my background in district roles at the 'sharp end' of things rather than being seen at just a policy bloke in the ivory tower of head office.

The income job gave me my first real experience of project management as at the computer centre I was working on projects being led by someone else and I had not initiated them in the first place. The breadth of cover of customer accounting polices meant that there were a number of opportunities for new projects that I would lead on.

One of the first of these related to county court judgements for outstanding debts. The company policy was that the district debt collection staff would pursue a debtor for any unpaid electricity bills up to the point when it was decided that court action would be necessary. At this point the case would be handed over to the head office legal section where court action would be taken by the company under the name of the company solicitor. Some recent legislative changes meant that debts could be pursued in the Small Claims Civil Court and this could be carried out without the services of a solicitor. It was proposed that this work could be transferred back to the district debt collection staff instead of the legal department who, from memory, would only become involved at the later enforcement stage. I won't go into the details here as I am not sure I clearly remember them but essentially I was being placed at the centre of a turf war between two deputy chief officers at head office. The company solicitor who was the deputy Company secretary and Bob, the deputy chief accountant, both considered to be rising stars and in their late thirties.This was a power struggle with only one winner and my meetings with them both separately took all my powers of diplomacy as I worked for one but the other was not one to make an enemy of. I do remember a certain amount of clandestine meetings including a couple with a retired member of the legal staff, set up by the accountant and who seemed to have a score to settle with the solicitor. There were also meetings with some district debt collection staff trying to convince them this increase in workload would be 'job enriching,' allowing them to pursue recalcitrant debtors into the courts rather than handing cases on to head office who they had previously criticised for being soft and slow. I think the compromise was to undertake a trial in one of the more enthusiastic districts but not before the solicitor had over a lunch tried to recruit me for his legal department. It didn't appeal to me and it caused some amusement to the deputy chief accountant, who said that we must have his opponent on the run if that was his answer. I think it was all part of a corporate game of moving work around in the name of efficiency savings whilst reducing department's head counts. After a successful trial the work was transferred to the districts a number of whom said it was satisfying to see more of their debt chasing achieving tangible results. For me it was one of my first (of many,) experiences of introducing something new to an often reluctant and suspicious audience.

One of the next projects was something different and brought me into contact with both the police and criminals. There was a term in the industry that was bandied about - 'System Losses.' In effect the amount of electricity bought of generators and put into the distribution system always fell short by some margin when it was metered, billed and paid for by customers. The major part of this figure which at the time was running at some 7 % of the total nationally was due to what were termed 'Engineering Distribution losses,' which were the losses of energy within the system due to heating of plant and transmission inefficiencies in plant and transformers. There were other smaller components of the total such as unmetered supplies but these could be calculated. It was known that this percentage was gradually improving in recent times due to network design and more efficiently operating plant but the total figure was not reducing. The difference was felt to be due abstraction, that is the theft of electricity, where meters were by-passed or tampered with. One board had set up a local sample study and believed their losses could be as high as 2 - 3 %. Most regional electricity boards were at that time billing on average £1 billion pounds so we were talking about possible thefts of 20 to 30 million pounds per company. Ironically, the boards in theory could ignore it and simply bill the customers who were registering consumption and the losses would be covered, I guess in the same way that honest shoppers cover the cost of shop-lifting. But the sample study suggested the thefts were increasing and in a number of cases the fire services believed that the by-passes had caused house fires and possibly fatalities. There was also interest from the police as illegal cannabis farms were often abstracting electricity to provide the quantities of light and heat that was necessary.

Often the industry umbrella organisation, the Electricity Council convened its members together to develop a unified response to matters of mutual interest and this was one such occasion. I was asked to attend to represent my Board and before I went I made contact with one of our own staff in Kent who had been working with the police in our area and had taken a number of successful prosecutions through the courts. The Kent guy was ex-police and had an evangelical approach to 'getting these b@@@@s who were getting free electricity which the rest if us were paying for.'

An interesting side note, pre nationalisation some electricity companies did provide free electricity to some of their workers; a similar benefit in kind, I was told, as miners received with their free coal. My Welsh roots are a little tenuous to the mining industry

126

although my paternal grand father worked in the 1950's as a clerk of works for the National Coal Board and was involved in the programme of pit head baths building. I am told this was a very welcome innovation both for the miners but also for their wives and families, as the coal-dust was now mostly left at work. As a child, the son of one of our neighbours worked for the coal board and I remember the pavement and part of the road being blocked with his regular free coal delivery which came in a big pile and not delivered in sacks like ours but I am sure it was much envied.

The meeting was interesting and some area boards were more aware of the problem than others but there was also a hard message from the electricity council member that there had already been some dialogue with the Home Office reminding the industry that they had an obligation of good governance which included the deterrence of crime. This had been reinforced with a veiled threat over government funding via the department of energy which was a message also being put out in relation to the industry finding and funding alternatives to coin operated meters as the 'thefts' from these although by customers in their own homes were inflating national crime figures. Perhaps for the first time I was gaining an awareness of the significance that the Income group could play in national socio-economic politics and issues.

 The delegates agreed at the end of the meeting to keep in touch with one another and to develop an exchange of good practices in this area. I had to report back to my own Board and it was agreed that the Income section would take a company wide responsibility for this anti-theft campaign. It was decided that we would transfer the guy from Kent to our section as he seemed to know more about this than anyone else in the organisation, certainly more than I did!

Part of the plan was for us to establish meter fraud teams in all the districts, monitor results and to develop best practices with Mike training staff and liaising nationally, as well as with the courts and the police. It was a move of the department to a more hands on , nitty gritty role and was uncomfortable for some of the head office staff. I recall a conversation with one of the accountants over reimbursement of monthly expense accounts which included a payment to the bar bill at a police social club. I think in future such claims were recorded as 'miscellaneous expenses' along with the advice that 'police informant payments' were best described as something else.

Our new recruit because of his police background habitually called me and other managers 'Guv,' and discussions with him made me feel I had a walk on part in 'The Sweeney,' or some similar TV drama. Our campaign was of genuine interest to the police as when warrants were obtained by us to enter a premises where we had evidence of theft or electricity abstraction, in the legal jargon, they would be keen to be in attendance if the suspect was a person of prior interest to them. Magistrates were often happier to issue warrants to the board as we could demonstrate reasonable grounds with reports from meter readers of broken meter seals or erratic consumption records. I attended a couple of 'raids' that were carried out but I was mostly content to leave Mike and some of his colleagues and the police to get on with it. Perhaps it was some sort of Melchett and Darling syndrome, safely back in HQ leaving our Blackadder, Baldrick and George at the front.

The initiative was a rich source of war stories some almost beyond belief.

After one warrant execution the defendant came up with an interesting counterclaim that although the meter had been 'fixed,' he had intended paying the electricity bill with a large amount of cash that was stored in a silver teapot kept on top of the meter but had mysteriously disappeared after our visit and his arrest. I was required to give a character reference for our 'callers' to confirm the board had no previous knowledge of crimes committed by them and to confirm that the said silver teapot was not in our possession - seriously!

Other dangers were guard dogs on premises and another instance of a large snake in a heated vivarium near the meter, (which wasn't recording!)

A more worrying event was an evening call to a Kent premises said to be the home of some notorious gangland figure when our team and the police were stopped in the driveway by some armed black balaclava figures flashing 'special branch' id's and they were asked to leave to avoid some other 'ongoing investigation.' The name later came up in some major drug crime case.

As well as reports from our meter readers we were becoming more sophisticated in analysing data that we already held about customers and premises. Around this time there were further developments in moving computer access away from the centralised data centre. With access via terminals in both headquarters and district offices one new application was a retrieval report software programme with the snappy title of 'Easytrieve' that allowed the interrogation of data files by users to produce bespoke reports. It can't have completely lived up to it's name as I recall going on a course of several days to gain a rudimentary knowledge of this. Nevertheless, it proved useful in providing reports for the meter fraud teams where combinations of suspicious consumptions combined with broken meter seal reports could be grouped into geographical areas for investigations. The result though were impressive and before long recovered billed losses board-wide were well into seven figures and the programme was deemed a success that even the shyest of head office accountants could cite as a good return on investment.

After several years working with Harry he took me to one side and told me he had decided to retire as the board were offering favourable severance terms to over sixties and he wanted to spend more time in Spain where he had a holiday home and access to golf courses with guaranteed sunshine, unlike Sussex.
He reassured me that he felt I was ready to take over the head of Income role and although the position would be advertised he believed that I would be successful. I wasn't so confident as I discovered that several qualified accountants had applied and they had been working in head office for longer and some of them were senior to me.
On the interview day I was surprised not to see Harry in the office we shared and he had still not appeared by mid morning when the Chief accountant's secretary collected me early for the interview. She had two items of information and I wasn't sure if either of them were reassuring. The first was that the previous interview had been cut short as one of the candidates had said something that upset the chief and the interview had been curtailed. The other piece of news was that Harry was on the interview panel which I could see was sensible but wasn't usual company practice and I wasn't sure if this would help me or not but it at least explained where Harry was. It was also known that the chief could be short-tempered and as the euphemism goes was not said 'to tolerate fools gladly'- which I always think is a strange metaphor.
Like many interviews, even later that day, it was hard to remember the details. I answered all the questions and the discussions were very detailed as was to be expected as one of the panel knew the role inside out! I was pleased when it was over and I think my ambitions about getting the job were as much about who would replace Harry, who I respected and

130

enjoyed working with, if I didn't get the job. At lunchtime I took a long walk along Hove seafront to clear my head and brace myself for any news later that afternoon. A restless couple of hours later I was called into the chief accountant's office to be greeted by him smiling and shaking my hand with a grinning Harry sitting next to him.

"We are pleased to offer you the Head of Income position - we both think your are the best candidate." He then added darkly, with the smile temporarily leaving his face, "unlike one of the candidates you haven't underestimated the challenge of the role - he peed me off so much with his arrogance of how it would do for the time being it was all I could do to stop physically throwing him out. Anyway, onto happier things, Harry has always told me you are the best candidate so that's all of us happy."

The promotion was very welcome as it was two grades above my previous one which I had held for a couple of positions so I was very pleased and it helped out with the extensive building works we were carrying out on our beloved flint cottage, dragging it into the twentieth century with an extension, new bathroom, new roof, insulation and central heating.

My gaining promotion meant that I needed to recruit someone into my old post and the increasing emphasis on customer policies and improvements meant we could also increase the permanent establishment of the section so I had two vacancies to fill.

I was fortunate that one of the applicants was a fellow secondee to the computer planning section and since that time Bill had managed customer sections in one of the Sussex districts so was a credible addition to the team. The other new recruit was 'poached' from one of the other head office accounting sections, Kevin a bright qualified accountant, a couple of years younger than me and very skilled with figures, financial appraisals and computer spreadsheets. It was becoming more and more important that our policy proposals were supported with sound financials and this recruitment certainly helped with this. Together with Mike and Tom our new team was complete. Tom was another qualified accountant who had grown up in Ghana and having moved to the UK as a young adult in the big freeze of 1963, at the time wondered if he had made a mistake! He was our English grammar expert and we would always get him to cast his eyes over and press releases or publicity material from grammatical accuracy. It was a happy group and we regarded ourselves as an outlier in the finance department perhaps because we needed to be more attuned to the customer needs of the world outside rather than just numbers.

One example of this was our response to a Christmas sherry party invite that had been extended to senior managers by one of the snootier department managers. In the 1980's home brewing was at its height in the UK with Boots the chemist having large home brewing departments in their larger stores. Here you could buy all that was necessary from yeast, hops and malt ingredients to barrels and bottling supplies. I had experimented with both beer and wine at home, although I didn't claim any great success and the results were often only palatable with the addition of a top up of lemonade.We had some particular disappointments with our elderberry wine which had a medicinal quality about it, and not a good one. This was particularly disappointing as our Sussex cottage garden had an ample supply from a number of elderberry bushes that the previous owner had let grow into large trees. We did have some success with an old recipe for elderflower champagne that was made in a similar way to home made ginger beer. I am not sure whether it was alcoholic but it's effervescence had a similar euphoric effect to real champagne. Unfortunately, this quality led to one explosion at home in the pantry where the expansion was strong enough to strip the thread off the recycled lemonade bottle and had made quite a mess when we

132

discovered it. The experience was not quite so alarming as that for two friends that we had given a bottle to. Their explosion occurred in their small two seater sports car on their drive home to Brighton and I still feel bad about this, so sorry Sue and Kelvin and I recall them telling me the elderflower smell lingered in the car for some time.

Back to the sherry party; it seemed that Kevin had developed more brewing expertise than I had and had extolled the virtues of one particular home brew brand that had the splendid name of 'Bruce's Brewery Dogbolter.' It also boasted an alcohol proof in excess of 7% when lagers if that period were closer to 3 or 4 %. So some weeks before Christmas a brew was set up in the corner of our office next to a nice warm electric storage radiator and at the designated time, rather than the laborious process of bottling, the brew was placed in a large home brewers plastic barrel to finish the process. Invites were quietly given to selected members of staff to drop around mid morning for the Income section's pre Christmas drinks whilst given assurances that they would have plenty of time to go onto the traditional sherry drinks party. We were not generous enough to provide any crisis or biscuits to accompany the rocket fuel so by lunch time there were reports around the building of people sleeping off the effects in quiet corners, complaints of some arrivals to the sherry party already drunk and other reports of cars being left in the office car park overnight as the revellers sought alternative means if transport home. We had taken the precaution of travelling into work that morning on the train so Bill and me were amused to meet several colleagues from the soirée who were blearily taking unexpected train journeys that evening. The celebration was never repeated but the event was talked about at subsequent christmases.

Another incident was related to a news event of national significance. In October 1984 the IRA exploded a device in Brighton's Grand Hotel being used by delegates to the Conservative Party conference. Margaret Thatcher was thought to be the intended target but escaped the blast which killed five and injured another thirty four victims. Our offices in Hove were further west on the seafront and out of morbid curiosity a few of us walked along the front to sea the damage. Even though the blast was some hours earlier the scene was still one of organised chaos with emergency services, onlookers, TV crews and press near the extensively damaged building.

Barriers had been set up but with a fear of further collapse of the building there was an effort by the police to extend the security zone away from the building.

At this point I should explain that my colleague, Bill was a tall, dignified man with a kind of military bearing and a commanding presence from his stature. We were wearing our business suits and I think Bill wore a dark, military style mac. I was suddenly aware that a young fresh-faced constable was addressing us, or more specifically Bill, asking "how far back should we move the crowd barriers, Sir?" Quick as a flash Bill vaguely pointed some yards away and airily stated "I think that should about do it, constable."

Having seen the site of the disaster we wisely left the scene before getting involved in any more complex arrangements or being asked to 'help the police in their enquiries.'

ICL Interview.

Strangely, at a time of plentiful jobs, company takeovers and expansion and new companies coming into being created, I didn't really suffer much career restlessness. New opportunities had occurred within the company over the years so it was a little out of character to apply for a position with another company. The opportunity was with ICL, at the time one of the country's largest   IT companies and supplier of software and hardware to government, local authorities as well as to the utilities. At the time our company was using IBM equipment but amongst the UK electricity companies the split was shared between ICL and IBM. ICL was anxious to grow it's share of the market and was looking to recruit from within the electricity industry to better understand the needs of the industry. The initial interview was in London, after which I was shortlisted for a follow up interview at their Thames valley offices which would service the electricity industry client base. I must have been seriously considering the job as we actually explored the villages near the offices one weekend as a preliminary 'speculative house hunt.' This was in the days before the internet with local newspapers and estate agents listings being the source of potential moves. We had already discussed moving to the country from Worthing and a job move could help with the cost of this.

Between the two interviews I took the opportunity to admit to my chief officer that I had this second interview and he quizzed me whether the provision of a company car was a factor in my restlessness. I admitted that it was playing a part and he said that I should exclude this from the equation and dropped heavy hints that suggested a company car might be forthcoming for me soon.

In the event by the time of the second interview I was having doubts about the move as house prices in the area were at least as expensive as Sussex and the second interview seemed to concentrate more on the sales aspect of the job, an area that I felt I had no proven abilities in. I was saved from having to make the decision when the job was offered to someone from London Electricity that I had worked with on some national working groups.

I don't know if the incident had any influence but a few weeks later I was offered one of the holy grails of corporate life - the company car. This was very attractive, no more worries about passing MOT'S or buying new tyres or even more expensive mechanical bills. We were to become a two car family again which was welcome as we were in the process of moving from a town to a much more rural location the dream cottage in the country complete with space around us - a big garden and attached meadow with bridle and

footpaths through neighbouring woods. There was even village pub some two miles away through the lanes.

More contemporary photos at https:// linkcottage.home.blog/

Sadly the brand new car wasn't going to be a Jaguar or a Volvo, nothing quite so exotic. At the time my employer was a nationalised industry and there were policies for everything, (some of which to my shame I had authored - still it was a living and apparently somebody had to do it!) The policy was clearly written in an attempt to reduce the unalloyed joy of spending thousands of pounds of someone else's money - in this case the electricity customers in the south east of England - I reckoned most of them could afford it after all it was the most affluent part of the the country.

Rule 1 - Uk recognised manufacturers only, by this they stipulated Ford, Vauxhall and British Leyland, (no mention of Jaguar, Bentley or Morgan) and certainly no Ferraris or Maseratis.

Rule 2 - nothing too fancy or exciting so no 2 door coupes, convertibles, or 4 x 4's.

Still, it was the first new car I would own and it wasn't going to be my money I was spending. Research was done with car magazines and brochures and as luck would it have it that weekend there was a manufacturers car show on the sea front in Sussex. It was decided I would attend along with our fully grown Irish Wolfhound, Rollo some thirteen stones of hair and muscle wrapped up in a still puppyish temperament. We were definitely in the market for another estate car although the ones on offer from the designated approved suppliers were a lot smaller than the Volvo estate he was used to. We looked first at the Vauxhall stand where the offerings were between an Astra or a Cavalier estate. Where or how do car manufacturers dream up their model names. I would have expected the Cavalier to have some frills on the seat or at least an integral hatstand to hang your large floppy hat up on. In truth the choice would have been between the top of the range Astra (which seemed tinny and tiny after the Volvo, or the bottom of the range Cavalier which lacked the hatstands and was a bit dreary.) In the event they took themselves out of the running by refusing to let Rollo try out the rear space for size, citing his hairiness. The sales man was rewarded by the dog pushing him in the bum with his wet nose when he had turned his back on us to securely close the rear door. We moved on to the Ford stand where the Escort estate was immediately dismissed as being too cramped and the only other choice was the Sierra estate.

The Sierra was something of a radical change for Ford and initially had been criticised for it's 'jelly mould' shape which was a departure from the more angular designs common throughout the 1970's and 80's. Influential in the concept design was Patrick Le Quément who will reappear later in my story of ownership of extreme cars.
(The Tracks of my Tyres -Amazon books.)
Ford helped their cause by allowing Rollo to jump in the back of the estate car on display and the salesman tried to capitalise on this by announcing to onlookers that the estate car could even accommodate a monster dog. Of course Rollo was not over helpful by demonstrating there wasn't really enough room for him to sit up straight so shuffled about sending clouds of dog hair to decorate the interior and causing the car to rock alarmingly from side to side until I felt sorry for both of them and persuaded him to lie down, the dog that is. Which he did with his front legs hanging out the back further belying claims of roominess. I persuaded him to jump out and thanking the salesman moved next door to the British Leyland stand where the salesman was hastily closing all the

doors and boot on his Montego estate having observed the antics on the Ford stand next door. Rollo was bored now and dragged me past this over to a food stall where we both enjoyed a hot dog. As some of his was left in his beard I concluded it was probably time to leave thinking that it looked like we would be ordering a Ford Estate car unless I could persuade the company to supply me with a company Land Rover or Van.

The company car arrived some weeks later a 1.8L estate car in standard white with a sunroof as the only extra. Quoting from a manufacturer's sales brochure of that year:- "The Sierra L is a very significant model because it brings Ford's new 1.8 engine into this range. Launched at the same time as the standard setting 1985 models this state of the art power unit features the latest in 'lean burn' technology for superb economy plus a very strong dash of sporting flavour. Crisp acceleration and a top speed of 110 mph are one side of the coin. On the other, the 1.8 with its standard five-speed gearbox gives an official 47.1 mpg at 56 mph."So take that Greta Thumberg - in

1985 manufacturers were becoming hyper sensitive to fuel economy issues!"

The brochure goes on to extoll further virtues:-"Its high technology features also include an electronic ignition system and a twin choke Pierburg carburettor with electric inlet manifold heater controlled by a spark module for cold starts."All very high tech then and with a space age blobby shape! My memory of ownership is pretty positive and I don't remember any particular problems with it. I did complain to the company transport department about an intermittent rattle/scratching sound below the dashboard. They offered to look at it when I next needed a service but the problem solved itself when I spotted a mouse in the passenger footwell who was snacking on the crumbs of my mid-drive snacks. I was more careful about leaving the doors open when parked near the supplies of duck corn in the garage which was the main attraction for mice in our garden.

I only remember two repairs. The first was the replacement of one of the back windows after taking a corner rather enthusiastically and pitching a large metal container carrying a projector that we had been using in some post SE England 1987 Hurricane presentations as a company PR exercise. This was a minor problem when the car could have been totally written off by the same storm when several huge trees had crashed down in our garden near both our cars. The second was when I borrowed an industrial strength jet washer from the maintenance engineer at the office to give the car a good spring clean after a winter of driving in the muddy Sussex lanes. All was well until I directed the powerful jet of water onto the front panel of the car that must have been plastic and as I played the jet across it the panel started to change colour from white to grey as the paint was stripped off. My long suffering corporate transport department arranged a respray for this faulty paint job that I was keen to lay the blame on Ford's poor quality paint. A true white lie.

140

Rollo choosing his estate car

There was one drawback though - Rollo did fit in the back of the car- just, but for longer journeys his moving about in the back of the car made the car more unstable than felt safe so for weekend trips from Sussex to Wales, when he was present, we still used the trusty old Volvo estate that seemed heavy and stable enough to cope with his fidgeting. Oh, and I remember one other potential problem in that the car had proved to be popular with high sales volumes so that it wasn't always easy to find in a car park in among several others. Also locks being less sophisticated than nowadays I once found that I had unlocked and got into 'my' white estate car to find someone had already broken in and left a briefcase and umbrella on the back seat! Getting out quickly I found my car several spaces away and unlocked it and escaped before potential arrest as a car thief.

Working at head office widened my horizons both figuratively and physically as there were national working groups that called for representation from the regional boards on a range of issues. The meetings

141

were mainly arranged at the Electricity Council's offices in Millbank Tower, overlooking the river Thames and between the Houses of Parliament and the Tate gallery. It felt a long way away from a boy having grown up in Swansea but the right place to be discussing   and perhaps solving some of the national issues facing the industry. Normally, the meetings were for one day but because some of the representatives had longer journeys than I did, the hours were very civilised, rarely convening before 10.30 and finishing before 4 p.m. If I didn't catch the train straight back to Sussex there was time to meet friends working in town or to shop or visit a gallery. All in all very civilised and in this job and in other roles I was always happy to represent the company at these and similar meetings.

Over the years I represented the company on a number of issues, some were closely related to my function and responsibility, some less so and often new and yet to be anyone's clear responsibility. I seemed to have gained a reputation for involvement in new areas and an ability to pick things up quickly and appear at least half way sensible. At least that's the positive story, I may have just been good at b********ting and happy to travel to the city for the day, but I certainly enjoyed working groups on a wide range of topics with the more obscure including carbon tax, emf emissions, the single market, to the more relevant privatisation and customer regulation and energy bill estimating. It was also a time of rapid change for the energy industry and I had always hoped to be part of those designing the changes rather that being passive or having change inflicted on me. It all seemed a long way from the first morning sitting in the reception hall in the Folkestone office having surprised everyone with my unexpected arrival.

The job also gave me my first opportunity for international travel and at the company's expense. It seemed that every couple of years a small French independent utility held a conference over several days in their city in the French-German border. I had never heard of this or knew anyone who went to it but for some reason the invite to Seeboard was resisted by the chairman, chief accountant and his deputy and it was suggested that as the conference was about customer matters I should be our nominated attendee.

I flew from Gatwick on an early morning flight the day the conference was due to start with an evening reception. The scheduled flight was fairly empty but I was surprised by a short stop at a small municipal airport in northern France, where a number of french guys boarded who seemed to be from EDF and were going 'mob handed.' They ordered beers, it was only 10 am and as I had been chatting to them in a mixture of my schoolboy french and their broken English I was included in the drinks order. It was all very convivial and I couldn't help thinking maybe I should be back in the office having my second coffee of the day. I checked my bag into the hotel and had a wander around the city which had nice shops, wide streets and some riverside cafes and restaurants. The city was very picturesque and a mix of medieval buildings and modern shops. I remember that although the day had started sunny by mid afternoon I was caught in a rain shower and bought myself an umbrella.

The evening reception was not far from the hotel but the organisers had arranged for a fleet of cars to ferry delegates to it. I found myself in a car with three Scottish delegates who seemed surprised I was there by myself from our company and were happy for me to tag along with them. Inside the reception there seemed to be hundreds of people, many from EDS (Electricity de Strasbourg,) and I was later told this 'show of strength' and the conference itself was something of a snub to their much larger and state owned neighbour EDF. There was a delegates list handed out along with a schedule of events with the promise that more papers and materials would be given out the next day.

Scanning the list I saw that I knew a couple of other delegates from past Income managers national groups but also there were many senior board members from the UK and other countries. I also found out that one of the speakers on a remote metering trial was from my own company and he had been away working on a secretive project, I would meet Derek later.

There was a formal seating plan so I said goodbye to my new Scottish friends, one of whom had the surname Smiley and I already had mentally christened them as 'Smiley's People'.

We had been given name badges with names and companies shown. At the table the guy next to me asked what I did and after I gave a short description asked him the same -"very little - I am the deputy chairman," followed by mutual laughter. I realised it was going to be an enjoyable few days.

The rest of the week passed pleasantly with a mixture of good food and drink, interesting presentations and some entertainment including an evening dinner on a river boat going up, (or down - I didn't check which,) the Rhine. A sort of beer Keller supper in an old medieval mint building as well as lavish multiple course luncheons. I was glad of the copies of notes for the presentations as I was sure I would need these to justify the learning experience back at the office.

Around this time there were some senior staff movements in the company with the Board's company secretary replacing the retiring Chief Accountant and his deputy leaving the organisation to be replaced by our boss, Chris. For a few months Chris's position was temporarily filled by a line manager from one of the districts. This worked to our advantage as he had first hand knowledge of customer accounting at the 'sharp end' and saw a kindred spirit in me as I had started my career in district. It was a useful lesson in delegating upwards as Fred often proved useful in presenting corrected mistakes or controversial proposals to Chris as he was viewed as a 'wise head' with current knowledge of customer behaviour. Unfortunately, this happy state of affairs wasn't to last as he was permanently replaced by a younger accountant apparently head hunted from a neighbouring local authority. In a short time it was concluded by us that this new man must have been gifted in one solitary skill and that was the art of the interview. He was hopeless and offered little in the way of management and was soon discredited across the company. This wasn't helped by him using his time with us as a sideline to his 'self-build' house project. Colleagues in our other offices would delight in spilling the beans on this endeavour by phoning us to report his late arrival in their car park with lengths of timber on the roof rack of his company estate car, obviously having detoured to their meeting by way of his builders merchant.

Leaving Head Office

Something of a pattern seemed to be occurring in my career. Just as I had settled into a role and could be considered to have 'got the hang of it,' and maybe felt less under pressure, a new opportunity presented itself and I couldn't resist taking it. In this case it was a short physical move about two miles to the west from the Hove head office to the district office of south West Sussex. The customer service officer (CSO, yes we still loved acronyms,) had taken a secondment and the divisional manager was looking for a temporary replacement. I don't know what part the the friendly verbal debates that were a regular feature of my relationship with Chris, my manager, played in the suggestion but I like to think it was a helpful career move he was arranging for me. He had suggested to the district manager that I had the necessary experience and skills for the role and that it would be an opportunity for me to refresh my practical skills away from the policy role and also give me an enhanced management experience. I met the DM with Chris, both of whom said flattering things about me, how useful I would be to the district, how much Chris would miss me and how he needed me to help him recruit a temporary replacement. The worst thing was telling my team of Tom, Bill, Kevin, Mike and Nick. Their reaction was predictable, after the few years together we were all getting on well and our initiatives and developments were enjoying success. We had developed a good relationship with our counterparts in the districts and they didn't really understand my decision to leave the centre to go to what they saw as a more peripheral role, even temporarily. The probable truth was that I was getting bored and fancied a change and the chance to do something new in a different environment and I thought it was a low risk option with, in effect a return ticket. Fortunately, we were able to persuade another well-respected section head, Mike, to make the move from one of the finance departments where Kevin had previously worked with him. This went some way to alleviating their fears over my departure and gave me some comfort that the department would be in safe hands for my anticipated return.

Hurricane

I arrived in my new job at the end of September 1987 and had hardly settled in when on the night of October 15th an unprecedented event took place. It has entered the annuls of broadcasting by way of Michael Fish's weather forecast that evening when he reported that a woman had phoned in to say that a hurricane was on it's way and he assured viewers by saying this wasn't the case. He was wrong- oh, so wrong!

We had moved to the country earlier the same year and our new home was in the High Weald near the border of Kent and East Sussex. It was an idyllic position with a huge garden and uninterrupted views to the hills of the South Downs some twelve miles away. That evening we became aware of the penalty of this exposed position as we experienced the first really windy night in the home. That night the loft hatch lifted up and down and the water level in the toilet was siphoning up and down. Strange I said as we went to bed and both slept right through until I awoke without the help of the bedside clock radio alarm. Waking I could see that the electronic display was blank and realised the power was off. The mystery deepened as looked at my watch and found it was after 8 o'clock. We had overslept and although we were in a rural location the road outside, particularly at this time would have a regular flow of traffic but it was silent. In the bathroom I switched on a battery radio but could only get static.

I then said that I would be late into the office which was almost an hours drive away so tried to phone to tell them this but the phone was dead. My wife had drawn the curtains and said the garden looked different - we were starting to get alarmed, outside it was eerily quiet and our dog had gone into the garden and was barking loudly, Again this was strange as he was a large Irish Wolfhound with a laid back temperament and it normally took something unusual to startle him, like a hot air balloon or a car backfiring.

Walking out into the garden I went through the gate into the kitchen to find the dog barking at the foundations where yesterday we had a greenhouse, of which there was not sign but I could see some shards of broken glass on the ground. So grabbing him by his collar I coaxed a reluctant Rollo back to the house where I met my wife coming out saying in an anxious tone - "the ponies - are they ok." We had acquired the temporary loan of two ponies from the local riding school who had a grazing arrangement with the previous house owners and which we had continued in exchange for free riding lessons.

She ran down the path to where the stable was, a grand title for a large wooden shed, a loose box is the term I believe. "Come quickly," she called and together we opened the top split half of the stable door fearing the worst as the stable had blown off its foundations and moved some ten foot or so, until the large hedge had stopped further movement.

Thankfully, Malcolm and Cupid, (not my names but they were veterans of the riding school,) were unharmed and pleased to be let out into the meadow where I also found the frame of the greenhouse some fifty yards from where it should be.

All the time I was wondering what had happened with the more extreme thoughts ranging over a nuclear attack or a meltdown explosion at Kent's Dungeness nuclear plant to who knows what. We had several large conifer trees down in the garden, tiles off the house roof and going out of the drive I could see that the A road outside was blocked in both directions by a number of fallen trees. Further up the road after clambering over the fallen trees the wires and telegraph posts in the road explained the lack of the phone service. We said hello to some other puzzled looking people in the road who we didn't know but having only moved a few months before had not yet met everyone in the tiny hamlet that was ambitiously named 'Little London.' Later that day after a few hours assessing the damage and carefully collecting up as much of the shattered greenhouse glass as we could we were surprised to here the first vehicle noise of the day. A noisy engine could be heard getting nearer, accompanied by thumps and metallic grating. This was accompanied by occasional bursts of what my few months of country living had allowed me to recognise as the high pitched whine of a chainsaw motor. As the noise came nearer our drive we went out onto the road to see a couple of high-viz dressed workers with chainsaws accompanying a tractor with a kind of bull-dozer attachment that was being used to push the fallen trees and telegraph poles to the roadside giving a single clear path down the road. They told us they had come from the council depot in the village to the south and were planning to clear the road north to our nearby market town. They recommended not trying to use the road for a few hours and if we do, to take care as some of it would be single file. We asked what had happened and they said they had been told a state of emergency had been called by the council and much of the south east was without electricity and the phone network was very restricted too. They had been told that hurricane force winds had hit northern France and South East England in the night and the storm damage was extensive over a wide area with possibly millions of trees blown down blocking roads and rail lines as well as bringing down power cables and phone lines. I could imagine the effect this chaos would have brought to the electricity operations and realised I needed to attempt to get to the office, some 35 miles away, as soon as I could. By mid afternoon after we heard a few cars slowly going past the house we drove slowly up the road. The council workers had cleared a path through the debris but the number and size of the trees meant that for much of the route it was a single track and when the few other cars came one of us needed to reverse so it was a slow journey. The small town was uncharacteristically quiet and the

few shops that were open had small queues outside them. After parking we could see why as the town was without electricity, tills and card machines were inoperable and shops were only allowing individual customers in to shop by torchlight. I don't remember what we bought, a few essentials I think, to be paid for by cheque and some torch batteries although the iron monger was sensibly rationing customers to a couple of these each. I queued outside the public phone box for quite a time and I think the people before me were having difficulty getting connected. When my turn came I tried the office switchboard which as I had anticipated was engaged. I remember my newly printed business card for my new role quoted my direct line extension number which was so new to me I had yet to memorise it. The line was answered by Derek who I had temporarily replaced. He explained it was pretty chaotic there but field staff were building a picture of damage across the county because our private mobile radio telephone network was still working and the office and some of the depots were operating on reduced power with back up generators. He said he understood that the county's road network was impassable in many places, even in urban areas. There was a skeleton staff who had got into the office that morning and a system emergency had been declared. I agree that as it was already starting to get dark it would make sense to attempt to get to the office the next day and he warned that it may be worth bringing spare clothes as I may not get home the same day.

The journey to work the next day was not straight forward. Without access to road traffic reports I had to guess which routes were open but there was some help where the council highway folk had put signs and barriers across

Our road in Sussex

seriously blocked roads. My normal route to Hove and Brighton was through a series of country lanes in effect cutting the corner off the north-south and east-west A roads. I drove south expecting to be able to cut across to pick up the A27 east-west road but kept coming across blocked routes. Even the main A road down to the coast was closed after a few miles so I cut across west and hoped on of the lanes were open. All along the route there was the high note sounds of chainsaws. The route I chose was just passable, although the driver of a car coming in the other direction told me there were still many trees on the road but it was just possible to drive around them if you didn't mind getting your car

The Level, Brighton

muddy on the roadside verges and banks. When at last I reached the A27 I was redirected back east and eventually after a long detour reached the cliff top coast road. Here instead of fallen trees there were houses and other buildings with their roofs torn off and some caravans blown over onto their sides. Many gardens had flattened sheds and greenhouses and although the wind had dropped the sea still looked rough. Every now and then the car tyres crunched over broken glass in the road and I expected to get a puncture any time. The route on the coast was blocked before Brighton so I was rerouted back over the downs to come down to the seafront as the route around Brighton to Portslade was also closed. Although traffic had been light the normal 45 minute

152

journey had taken almost two hours. I didn't see a working traffic light in town so each junction needed extra care. As I drove towards the seafront I could hear the noise again of chainsaws and at the Level, a park in the centre of Brighton, workmen were busy sawing up huge trees and I was directed around them to drive on the wide pavement. A policeman stopped me

and suggested it was dangerous to be out because if falling tiles and masonry and asked if it was an essential journey. When I showed him my Seeboard ID card and said I needed to get to the office in Portslade to manage the customer call centre he helpfully made a radio call and suggested the best route for me.

The sea front didn't have any trees to be damaged but I saw a number of damaged roofs and several cars flattened under piles of bricks and masonry where the wind had ripped off the sides of buildings. The seafront buildings must have taken the full brunt of the storm and many had damaged windows. I later heard in the office from a colleague that she had got up in the night in her sea front flat to look at the storm and as she opened the door to her sitting room the storm blew out the complete frame and glass of her flat frontage, it must have been terrifying. When I got to the office at last I found that the car park had less than half the usual number of cars in it. I was welcomed at my desk by a bleary eyed Derek who

153

said he had only managed a couple of hours sleep, on the floor of the office. He handed me a clip board with the names of staff who were in and some details of the rota system that had been set up to cover the customer phone lines. We briefly discussed the arrangements that had quickly been put in place yesterday to capture information of customers who were off supply. There were arrangements to collate the information into areas and run it at intervals into the engineering control room where the engineering staff were trying to make sense of the state of the network and prioritise repair crews to reconnect the maximum number of customers. Management meetings had been set up for 7 p.m. and 8 a.m. and he said I would gain a better overall picture that evening. We agreed that I would stay overnight as it was now mid-morning and we would meet again at the next day's 8 a.m. review. As he left he opened the desk drawer and pointed out a half empty bottle of spirits and recommended that it may help me sleep later as my bed would be the floor!

Talking to staff it was clear that people were having great difficulty travelling, even in suburban areas and the disrupted rail network was not helping. It was clear that many customers were off supply and the lack of phone lines meant that many more weren't able to advise us of the situation. Some office staff were being despatched in cars to make some on the ground assessments where possible in rural areas but often they came back reporting the kind of road closures I had seen on my disrupted journey that morning. It was clear that despite plans being in place for system emergencies the scale of this was making things very difficult. Normal office work was suspended and all resources were concentrated on assessing the scale of the problem.

Early on tensions surfaced between the district and Head Office who were trying to assess the situation across the whole of the south east to satisfy information requests from central government, the media and press as well as other local agencies. It was clear that this was not going to be any sort of 'quick fix.'

An overview of the task is shown on a video still available on YouTube -"Seeboard - Hurricane force '87." This gives some idea of the scale of the operation. It was clear, even in the first days, that the scale of the repair job was beyond our own resources, so calls were made nationally to other electricity boards who had not been affected by the storm and after the first weekend teams of linesman began to arrive in the south east from the north of England, Scotland and Ireland. The assistance was very welcome but with it came other logistical challenges in deployment, working methods alignment and the mechanics of accommodation and so on.

Arrangement for the teams helping us in Sussex were made with seafront hotels in Brighton and Hove with the council and police helping by turning the seafront promenade into one long car park overnight for the vans, lorries and land rovers with their different regional liveries.

Some specific amusing instances have stuck in my mind from those weeks of intense work and some of those served to lighten the mood at a difficult time. The first one I remember was when we sent some of our office staff to collect any spare batteries and torches in our shops and to drive out to remote areas where supplies were off and knock on doors and hand them out to customers.

I don't know if people were more tolerant or better behaved then but even at the time it seemed something of a provocative gesture. I didn't hear of any adverse reactions so maybe people were shocked by public servants in suits randomly turning up with free gifts.

I almost had my own recreation of a Dad's army TV programme scene. Along with assistance from other electricity boards it was arranged that the army would help us out with the emergency. We were advised to

155

expect a detachment of troops from the Gurkha regiment to assist with clearing areas up country where the denser woodland was hindering line rebuilding. The restaurant chef kindly arranged to put one of his curries on the menu that lunch time, (I have since discovered that Nepalese food is not particularly highly spiced and probably a more sophisticated flavouring than what was served - but the intention was good.) I was told to expect the arrival of some 60 troops late morning and I was to welcome them and liaise with them and the operational engineers over their deployment. Around midday our receptionist rang me to say three huge army lorries had driven into our car park so I went to meet them. Their English officer shook hands and when I said we had lunch arranged in the restaurant he said in a clipped Sandhurst accent, "The chaps have been travelling from base for over three hours they'll need a pee first. I'll get them to follow you to the ablutions."

I walked briskly through reception and along the corridor to the gents with the deafening sound of dozens of uniformed Gurkhas marching at half speed in their heavy army boots following me. I opened the door into the gents toilet and fortunately had the presence of mind to stand to one side as the line marched past me into the relatively small toilet which would only hold a dozen or so men standing shoulder to shoulder. It says much for their discipline that when I shouted "Stop!" That they did before all five dozen of them trooped in. It brought to mind the Dad's army sketch where Captain Mainwaring is pinned to his office wall by the weight of all his men trooping into his small office.

Later in the week when taking time out of the office to do some field visits I met an elderly bungalow owner in his garden in one of the more remote wooded villages. He was pleased that his overhead supply line was being connected but admitted a brief worrying moment when earlier in the week he had been shocked to see foreign, uniformed soldiers hacking their way with their kukri machetes through the fallen foliage at the bottom of his garden. As an elderly retired veteran of armed conflicts in a campaign in the Far East he had a few worrying minutes until he spotted a Seeboard uniformed linesman with them. There had to be a lot of improvisation. One of the contributory factors to the damage was that in the days before the storm there had been heavy rainfall across the south east with the softened ground making the downing of trees more likely. These damp conditions made an unusual demand from the staff in the field -"we need dry socks - now." Many staff were working eighteen hour days in very demanding conditions so meeting such reasonable requirements were important for morale as well as health purposes. I remember a member of the Hove staff being despatched to the local branches of Millets, the outdoor clothing store, with a large bag of cash in notes to buy up as many thick woollen hiking socks as they could supply.

We also had to make sure food was available so as well as the staff restaurants in the district and head office in Hove cooking for extended hours contact was made with some larger pubs in the more rural areas and an 'open cheque account' agreed to give hot meals to any workers who arrived and claimed to be working for Seeboard on restoring supplies. There were rumours of some taking advantage of the arrangement but we didn't believe we were providing pub lunches to every unscrupulous farm worker in rural Sussex.

There was some debate, particularly in the early days whether the offices should be showing their lights as for the first 24 Hours because of the back up generators, along with hospitals and the buildings of the emergency services they were alone in darkened streets. It was concluded that although some

157

customers might be resentful it may be better to display a sort of 'beacon of hope' that there was at least some normality in a world turned upside down over night.

The board was fortunate that like the emergency services we operated a private mobile radio network for operational use but there were issues in communicating with the other teams of linesmen and engineers that had come to our area to help. I remember, late one evening over the last cup of strong coffee before my long drive home being shown one of the prototype mobile phones that had been loaned to us by, I think Vodaphone or BT. It was attached to a large battery pack but smaller than the ones demonstrated with briefcase type power packs. It was handed around until one of the number phoned his brother in Australia much to everyone's amusement. I would have liked to phone home but our home BT line in a rural area wasn't reconnected until some six weeks later. The phone was quickly switched off and returned to the District Engineer's desk. It was only a couple of years later that they became an essential part of business although I would often rue their invention when mine would start ringing as I switched it on as I got in my car just after 7.30 in the morning.

I took the time to research some of the statistics for the hurricane and the damage caused by the storm of October 87.

Wind speeds of over 100 mph were recorded across the south of England with the highest gust in the UK that night registered at 122 mph.

It is estimated that 15 million trees were downed, roughly one fifth of the timber in the south east. In our area there were over 3000 electricity poles blown down with 700 miles of cable and this cut off some 5,000 miles of our network. Initially 4 million customers were off supply and although 90 % were back on supply within 24 hours, tens of thousands were without supply for days and some for a couple of weeks. The whole engineering operational staff of the board numbered 4,000 and these were all deployed onto recovering the network. In the days following the storm we were supported by an additional 2500 staff from other electricity boards as well as several hundred army personnel. The Board also hired helicopters to supplement the industry's small number of their own helicopters and these proved invaluable in surveying and supplying the more inaccessible parts of the network.

The stores and supply chains had extreme demands placed on them with the volume of replacement plant required in the first week and a half equivalent to a year and a half of normal usage. This included 50,000 replacement fuses, over 700 miles of cable, several hundred mains transformers and 3000 plus wooden poles. This was sourced from far and wide including some from the United States. Over 100,000 customer phone calls were handled, although many customers were without a phone service for many weeks after the storm with BT having a network rebuild task of their own.

The hectic few weeks working in my new role in a new office was actually really helpful in getting to know people quickly and there was also a strong camaraderie in the district from working under such trying conditions to achieve such positive objectives. Some months later I was reminded of the sense of achievement at that time when with others we toured a 'roadshow' of a video telling the story of the hurricane and the efforts required in the aftermath to reconnect customers. The few evening sessions I presented to community groups, particularly those in the more rural areas, were well received and gave the staff presenters enormous pride in the achievements of the workforce. Sadly, as well as the casualties who lost their lives in the storm itself, two electricity workers were killed through accidents during the restoration works, emphasising to others the inherent dangers in this work.

It was my first taste of external corporate PR and was shortly followed by becoming a co-presenter on the monthly Electricity phone-in that we hosted on BBC local radio. For almost an hour listeners were invited to phone in their questions and queries on matters electric and myself and one of the senior engineers would do our best to give a sensible and hopefully reassuring reply.

Like many things in life the reality is often less glamorous than you think.

The BBC Radio Sussex studios were in a grand Victorian corner building in a pleasant part of Brighton but once past the panelled reception the studio upstairs was more like a cupboard that the two of us and the presenter virtually filled and when one of the reception staff brought the coffees in it was really crowded. The presenter was a pleasant young guy who was very competent and put me at my ease. The engineer for the first couple of months, John had been on the show before and was also very reassuring but it was after the first programme that he confided to me that we needn't worry too much about the customer calls as we had a kind of escape clause that if the conversation was getting contentious or heated we could say - "Yes well Mr/Mrs X that sounds very concerning and I will research that thoroughly back at the office and phone you with a full explanation so that we can properly sort this out."

But what he did say was the Chairman was an avid listener to the programme and had been known to be on the phone to the office straight after the programme if he disagreed with the answer or was particularly miffed about the complaint.

I said "So if we get back to the office by 3.30 and he hasn't rung up in the next two hours before we go home then we can assume he is happy?"

160

Apparently not, John said that if the chairman was out it at a meeting he would get his PA to record it for later listening, so you can't feel completely safe for a couple of days. After a couple of months I wondered whether the chairman's story was true as although I appeared in the phone-in for two years he didn't ever call. An interesting fact, the radio presenter was the son of Brian Johnston the famous cricket commentator and though he was very competent and has enjoyed a successful career in broadcasting and production its interesting that the BBC has a number of broadcasting dynasties.

It was interesting in talking to staff in the office that although many of them spent their days speaking to customers both face to face and by phone they felt the phone-in to be somehow daunting and I had trouble to get anyone to take my place so couldn't take those days in the month off from memory.

Many of the calls, although important to individuals were relatively easy to answer. Being local radio there was a sprinkling of eccentrics who were concerned about things ranging from the French nuclear power stations across the channel to whether it was more economic to leave your lagged hot water tank constantly heated. There was also a competitive element amongst some callers, for example we would take a call from a customer saying their meter in their hall makes a ticking noise. Within the next half an hour there was a sort of escalation from 'I can hear mine behind two doors,' to 'my neighbour can hear mine through the party wall !'

There was a similar experience over reports of street lights out of order -"off for two weeks - that's nothing the one on our corner went out he first week our son started school and he's at university now!" I exaggerate, but only slightly and it was always a mystery why these people waited for the monthly radio programme rather than just ring up our office. The lure of the glamour of the media I suppose, (is that why I was doing it?-worrying,) still it was an interesting experience.

After the excitement of the hurricane and the aftermath the role settled down to the more normal activities in a large organisation. I was the manager of a large number of staff, numbering several hundred and although the experience in the storm had helped me get to know many of the staff in a short time in the more frantic atmosphere of that time I was still was still aware that I could never get to know so many people in the way I could when managing small teams. The storm had helped establish some superficial credibility as the pressure in the early days had meant that I would regularly go out on the 'shop floor' and put on a head set and take customer calls, maybe for only half an hour but it helped dispel the idea this was some back room guy from head office in a suit. I also would say good morning to anyone and everyone, varying it with a "hello there," and if I was lucky enough to remember a name would add that. I was asked by one other manager how I had learnt so many names in the first couple of weeks and I pointed out that I was saying six or seven "Hello there's" to the occasional interspersed name.

Another tactic was to involve less senior supervisors in the recruitment process on the credible theory that they were closer to the work and also traditionally prone to criticising the candidates recruited by senior management. It was a valuable for team leaders to engage in the interview process from the other side of the table as well as freeing up some of the managers to have more time to manage.

Another 'experiment' was to replicate the team meetings that I held over lunches or coffee with my direct report managers to random collections of staff. I found the exercise very valuable once initial suspicions were suspended and at one a week for an hour with half a dozen staff each time it was going to take some time to get to all staff. I think this was one initiative that I was forced to abandon after a couple of months as we were experiencing a period of high staff turnover and the attendant pressure on performance on the phones and case backlogs led some of the managers and team leaders to resent the short absences of staff, though privately I wondered if there was some feelings of insecurity of me hearing 'tales out of school.' I promised to reinstitute the meetings when work pressure eased but to my regret I had moved on before this could happen.

At the end of the secondment time I was approached by the district manager to ask me if I would be interested in staying on permanently and I realised that I was still enjoying life at the 'sharp end' and felt there was more for me to achieve there. So my secondment ended as a permanent position and I was kept busy with a mixture of routine activities and projects. The offices were constantly being reconfigured and changed and with the electrics and computer/network cabling it wasn't a simple process. Although the building was less than twenty years old changes in workloads and working practices meant we were always shifting people and furniture around the building as well as constantly looking at ways of working more effectively. At one of the weekly management meetings it was agreed that increasing staff numbers in the credit control department meant that it made sense to relocate the whole department to an area on the ground floor from their current position in the customer call centre on the second floor.

This was likely to be unpopular with the staff as the second floor enjoyed distant views of the sea and people generally are resistant, at least initially, to change. It was agreed that I would have overall management of the project and at the outset I negotiated a budget with the finance department to provide new furniture.

It was in the early days of computerisation and was what had been called 'the paperless office,' but for the us there had been little consideration over the effect these changes had on working practices and office layouts. New computer terminals and printers had been placed on tables and desks designed for paperwork and cables and wires snaked dangerously off work surfaces. There was clearly an opportunity to make some improvement to this state of affairs. The first thing was to set up a small steering group comprising a number of staff from the unit and it was important to be representative so that a line manager, team leader and a credit control clerk were chosen to represent views. These were joined by an electrical engineer, a telecoms engineer and eventually an office furniture supplier once a tendering process had been completed.

This project became for me a lesson in managing change as there was a distinct lack of enthusiasm among the staff for this move and it was important to overcome this for staff morale and managements credibility.

The introduction of computer screens into business had raised a number of issues ranging from eye strain, seating ergonomics and light levels in offices among them. The company had made some attempts to address these needs with good quality office chairs and the provision of anti glare filters for screens and free eye tests and glasses on request. We had noticed that the second floor location of the office with large south facing windows did cause lighting difficulties at different times of the day and window blinds were used with a need for adjustment as the light changed. It was recognised that the new office needed to be designed for working with the new technology and lighting and cable management was at the heart of this. The new location was on the ground floor with windows facing north into the car park but it did make managing lighting less problematic.

The new office was eventually declared a success. Line staff worked with the supplier to choose furniture designed for use with pc's even visiting the factory to see the manufacture process and choose finishes. The clusters of workstations each with an integrated uplighter, privacy screens and acoustic sound proofing made for a clear, uncluttered environment. House plants and framed pictures were chosen by staff and the additional incremental cost was well worth it. The lighting gave a calmer working environment complemented by pastel painted walls -helpful in an office where phone calls could often be stressful. The district manager was so pleased with the design and staff reactions that the board Chairman was invited to see it and managers from other offices were encouraged to see it and copy the approach.

At a personal level I was also pleased as I had proved to myself that I could manage and deliver a project of a more physical nature - something that I had often avoided in the past.

It had also been an object lesson to me in how to overcome people's resistance to change through allowing greater involvement in the process and eventual design.

Return to Corporate Life

The organisation was going through one of the reorganisations that happened regularly. This time it was a rationalisation of the number of districts by merger with the inevitable reduction in management posts. There were the early publication of proposals to privatise the industry and the Board were also looking restructure to prepare for this. We were told that new skills as part of becoming a plc were required in corporate head office roles and there was mention of the new departments that would be required Among them were shareholder registry, electricity purchasing, forecasting, regulatory, treasury and business planning. An unusual exercise took place over a couple of weeks when all of the managers above a certain level were interviewed by a small panel consisting of the Chairman and his deputy. We were not aware what roles we were being identified for but instead the interview felt more like a subtle fireside chat about our career to date, skills we felt we had and any ambitions unrealised.
Shortly after this some initial management posts were announced including the Customer managers in the new merged districts. To my surprise I wasn't named as one, instead my position in Sussex was filled by a manager who had been unsuccessful in his application when I had initially been appointed the previous year. The regional companies were also having to accommodate a number of senior staff from the central Electricity Council in London that was being drastically slimmed down to become more of a trade body. My disappointment was echoed by a couple of other colleagues who had also been thought to be front runners for the district customer positions. I was fortunate that one of the new directors who had arrived from the Electricity Council took me into his confidence and told me I had been earmarked for one of the new corporate roles but he couldn't say which

and suggested I just kept my head down and awaited news. It was difficult keeping my own counsel while my managers kept telling me they were shocked too and asking what would happen to me. Fortunately, before too long I was called to head office on Hove sea front where in a large empty office I was introduced to a tall man in his fifties who said he would be the company's new director of corporate strategy and the chairman had recommended that I would be a useful manager to work for him on business planning in the new plc after privatisation. I thought it best to express some modesty and said that I wasn't sure I knew too much about business planning but he was reassuring saying that some training would be arranged and that my mix of district and head office policy experience together with my economics degree would be helpful. He even said that the chairman had described me as a 'safe pair of hands,' so I began to wonder whether he had been listening to the BBC radio phone-ins. I was told that eventually we would recruit a small number of staff to the business planning section but initially I would be working on the privatisation process with specific responsibility for managing our response to an efficiency study. More would be revealed next week but if I could handover quickly at district and find myself a room in head office I would be starting on this efficiency study soon. He also said that until there was some official announcement it would be best to be discreet about the role and just say I was moving back to head office.

This was another difficult goodbye to colleagues, with me not being able to tell them about my new position or what I would be doing and I didn't even have a new phone number or extension to give them. It did fell like a leap into the relative unknown but I was quite excited about the new opportunity even if I didn't know too much about what it was exactly.

After my handover in district I arrived back in head office and the admin team there found me an small upstairs office with a sea view. I explained that it would probably be temporary and expected some questions but they explained it was all a bit strange in the office with new arrivals asking for accommodation but having no details of staff numbers or who they would need to be physically near. Still I had a phone extension, a desk and a chair along with an empty filing cabinet that I didn't really have anything to put in. I resisted going around the large five story building and chatting with colleagues as I wasn't sure I could construct a reasonable explanation of what I was doing back. I had brought an early desk top pc and a printer back with me that I had been mostly using in district to monitor work levels and phone traffic but in the absence of anything else I spent a couple of days going through pc tutorials on software packages so at least I felt I was doing something. My unease over being 'interrogated' by colleagues even extended to taking sandwich lunches in my room or going out into Hove or Brighton. Luckily, this subterfuge didn't need to go on for too long as my new director, Terry phoned me and explained that the following week I should attend a meeting in London that was being called by the merchant bankers managing the privatisation for the government and we would learn more about this 'efficiency study' that was part of the process.

The following week I found myself in a large room at the offices of a bank in the City surrounded by scores of people the vast majority of whom judging from mine and other overheard conversations didn't really know what was going on and we were hoping that the handful of people at the front of the room would soon enlighten us.

As with many such presentations there there was a long preamble and setting of historical context with references to earlier privatisations of utilities including British Telecom and British Gas. I think those presentations took us up to the coffee break which gave a number if us the opportunity to ask ourselves what it a meant for us and what was going to be our roles in the process.

It was explained that the REC's as they were now christened, (a lovely new acronym for the Regional Electricity Companies) were different from the monolithic structures of BT and British Gas. Allegedly, to allow a 'level playing field there was to be an efficiency study undertaken by consultants that would provide the base for an initial price setting of electricity tariff annual increases known as RPI - X where RPI was the Retail Price Index and X was a single figure between 0 and 5 with 0 being assigned to the most efficient companies and 5 to the least. This would provide an incentive for the least efficient companies to reduce their cost bases.

Then we got to the point of interest for many of us. It was explained that teams of management consultants would come to each company for a period of some weeks or months and request information to establish the relative efficiencies of the different companies and it was suggested that each company establish a small team of experts dedicated to meeting these requests and gradually I could see how I was going to spend the next few months. It came back to me that earlier in my career in the Income job we had to respond to an MMC enquiry, (monopolies and mergers commission,) and I vaguely recall this being mentioned in the interview with the chairman. I had started to take notes now that I could see where this was leading and realised I would have to relay this information clearly when back in Hove. The next day when I told my director about the meeting he suggested that I go with him to brief the chairman about this so for the first time in my career I was in the chairman's office talking about something more complex than a single customer complaint letter.

It was agreed that I would need a small team and it was decided that there should be at least one accountant and some technical input from an engineer.

169

The chairman would talk his directors and ensure that at least two of the best people would be released for this crucial exercise.

A few days later I was joined by Jim and Robin, one younger than me the other slightly older. We knew each other but hadn't worked together before but having had the task described to them they both seemed enthusiastic and appreciative of the importance that the result could mean to the company.

We set up in a larger office and were told that secretarial support and any equipment necessary would be supplied to us. There was also mention that an 'advisor' from the firm of accountants retained by the Board to advise on privatisation and a meeting was arranged with him for later that week.

It was clear that although previous flotations had made some money for the public as new shareholders, (who remembers the ad slogan for the British Gas shares sale - 'If you see Sid -tell him....), the real money would go initially to the teams of advisors and brokers already taking their Mont Blanc pens from the folders of their Filofaxes. This was my first experience of meeting the clean cut, expensively educated and suited twenty something management consultants. Our advisor, Simon fitted the description and provided some more helpful details of the mechanics of the review and discussed our likely approach with us. It still seemed like the industry was now at the mercy of avaricious middle men playing Chinese whispers through a process causing unnecessary complexity but the realist in me and my new colleagues knew this was the game to be played and we weren't the ones setting the rules.

The key to success, so we thought, was to ensure we had good access to data in the company and to the people who could authenticate it and quickly provide answers to supplementary requests. It was clear that drawing comparisons between the 12 RECS would be difficult given their different demographics, histories

170

and geographies as well as the different investment decisions they had made over the years. We knew that Seeboard had one of the most extensive overhead networks with attendant commitments to repair from winter storms but had to answer the consultants contention that the recent 1987 Hurricane, mentioned here earlier, meant that much of this network was, in effect, new.

In talking about presenting our case we decided that simple top level messages would be important and spent some time with our management services colleagues who were ardent lovers of graphical presentations to clearly analyse data. The use of scattergraphs and comparison charts was going to be helpful in getting our case across over how relatively efficient we were as a company. There was also a need to analyse regional differentials in salaries driven by the competitive nature of the job market in the south east of England, Although the companies were still using a national grading structure the application of grades to similar roles was not uniform. All of this and many other factors made the project demanding and the most intellectually challenging of my career to date.

Another benefit that would help me in later roles was the exposure across the company that the review gave me. At regular meetings of the Board I presented updates on the review and at each the Chairman or my new director would emphasise the significance that a good outcome would mean for the company and that it was vital that support should be given to me and my team in gathering information to support our case.

One amusing note to that time was that one of the new directors coming in from private industry, in the first week of his appointment, had tried one morning to get into see the Board chairman only to be told that he couldn't be disturbed at all as he was in conference with me. This went on for several hours as it was the first one-to-one meeting I had with the chairman to fully describe the process to him and outline and agree our approach. Later that afternoon the director's secretary was asked to summon this person he had never heard of to his office as I was clearly a person of enormous influence in the company. I had been warned about this new guy, his idiosyncrasies and high degree of status consciousness and his secretary warned me he had been very frustrated that morning and only just cooled down.

He was later to gain notoriety for his forgetfulness, the pinnacle of which was leaving the handbrake off his top of the range company car parked atop the white cliffs of Dover where it subsequently wrote itself off on the beach below. Some were heard to lament that it had been an unmanned flight ! That was all in the future.

He welcomed me in and mentioned that I had been with the chairman that morning when he had needed to see him. I apologised for that but said that when the chairman needed to see me it was impolite to refuse. He then went into an unsubtle conversation trying to find out what I had been talking to the chairman about, who I was, what my position was and who I worked for. I resented his quizzing so was quite evasive saying that I was working on special privatisation projects and the company structure was very fluid so he concluded that I was an external advisor, a conclusion I decided not to dispute. Even after several weekly meetings where I briefed the directors he was still operating under this misapprehension but it proved useful as he was far more polite to advisors than company employees and it was only later when he found out my true position that this pretence of civility was dropped after which we enjoyed a number of arguments but I was not alone in this.

The intensity of work on the Efficiency review ramped up when the team of four consultants arrive in the offices. In backgrounds we were a similar match with one accountant, an engineer and an economist. Their managing partner came for the introductory meeting but explained that the three would be in the Hove offices full time and he would only visit for reviews and updates. They were given an office near to ours and over the following weeks I am sure we all wore out a path in the corridor carpets between us. Colleagues in the company were helpful in providing the information we needed and there was a certain pride in demonstrating the benefits of initiatives that had been introduced to reduce costs or improve service. We received an 'intelligence benefit' part way through the project when for some reason one of the consultants asked for the use of a company desktop to reformat or print out a document, I don't recall which but whatever, it was the colleague in management services who alerted us to the fact that a copy still existed on our network. We couldn't resist printing it and found it was a draft of parts of their report on another of the REC's; the consultant teams were assigned to more than one REC. The draft helped us see where they were targeting their reviews and although we still needed to present good data of our own the windfall was certainly helpful. When I told our director about this he suggested the deputy Chairman should be told, maybe an example of sharing corporate responsibility. Not sure whether we would be criticised or congratulated I went to see him and found he was delighted and took it as a sign that our adversaries were human, but then said "I don't think too many people need to know about this."

Over the weeks of the review there were some late nights and like most pressurised projects the certainty that this process had a ultimate end point served to keep us going. The report was discussed in a number of fairly acrimonious meetings between us, the full Board and the team of consultants, with our side vigorously defending our comparative performance indicators and initiatives and the consultants proposing alternatives. At one point in one of the

173

meetings I leapt out if my chair to argue one point more forcibly and later after the consultants had left the room was congratulated by the board for my passion and asked if it was for theatrical effect - I replied that after the weeks of work building a case it was genuine and my acting skills are not that good. Eventually, a final report was received and commented on and some time later our regulatory formula was declared which was generally agreed as a positive result. The world of price regulation and its formulas became a science all of its own and thankfully I left the intricacies of this to others to worry about as I concentrated on recruiting a small team for my new department.

Business Planning

Recruiting for a new section in a newly formed directorate was always going to have its difficulties. There were lots of questions such as what would the work involve, what skills were required, what was the new director like to work for, what was I like to work for as a department head? So would recruitment be restricted to those disgruntled in their current positions, those worried about the longevity of their current role, or a new boss. The whole organisation was in something of a state of flux so certainties were in short supply. I had tried to learn a little more about business planning and in those pre-internet days had even resorted to the local reference library. Of more help was a seminar session arranged in London by one of the finance directors of a northern REC and coincidentally someone I had met earlier at the Strasbourg conference. The session was very helpful and gave me confidence as it was clear that some of the other newly appointed heads of this function were in a similar position as I was, trying to make sense of it. Two particularly helpful hints were firstly to read the book 'Practical Corporate Planning,' by John Argenti who I was to discover, was something of a guru in this new field of corporate science/art.
The second hint was there was a London based body called the Strategic Planning Society and a membership of this seemed to be a good idea.
I quickly arranged a subscription and with a combination of their journal, the Argenti manual and a healthy dose of confidence / optimism thought I was now enough of an expert to convince some recruits to join my new team.
I don't really remember many details but I think the role of Business Planning analysts was advertised with a sketchy description of the work and I had a few informal conversations with people I knew in the company. After the success of the privatisation efficiency study I had been given a promotion in grade

175

so I was able to present a picture that this might be an area of coming importance with promotion and growth opportunities.

One of the interviews gives substance to the fact that those were different times. I was to interview a candidate along with the outgoing head of management services who admitted the candidate was known to him.

After the interview we were discussing a candidate that we had just seen when the colleague said, "Well he's very able and bright but he is Welsh !"
Somewhat shocked, I interrupted and said -
'David, just let me say…..'
David carried on -"Well, I know I am stereotyping but they can be prickly and argumentative…."
I tried again to interrupt-
'David, before you say any more…'
But he was on a roll - "Some of them just have a chip on their shoulder and go out of their way to
….."
I couldn't take any more -
I loudly shouted -'DAVID - I AM WELSH.'
Undaunted he answered -
"Good God, are you? It doesn't show."
Anyway, we gave Alun the job - and he could be difficult but   not so much with me and we didn't refer David to the Race Relations Board,
different times!

So we had recruited my first team member, three more came by different routes but all in all I felt we formed a capable and enthusiastic team and were ready to face the challenges ahead. Unfortunately one of our greatest challenge was to come from an unexpected quarter - we were given a new manager as part of a flurry of recruitments around the time of privatisation to inject 'plc expertise' into the dozy world of nationalised utilities, at least that was the way some of the new blood saw it and our guy was no exception. In a short period of time he made enemies all over the company which actually worked to my advantage in that many of the directors and business heads would specifically ask that me and my team to work with them on their business plans and even make specific requests for this arrangement with my director.

In a vain attempt to raise team morale I asked my team members whether we could think of anything positive to say about our erstwhile boss. There was a long and embarrassing silence eventually broken by Alun reluctantly stating, "well, he's very clean." Although as we all agreed this was an irrelevant benefit in someone that much of the company's senior management were reluctant to meet with!

It was also Alun that had an eery experience one lunchtime. After a particularly frustrating dialogue in our bosses office Alun announced he was going straight out of the office for a lunchtime walk to clear his head. When I returned to our office after a quick lunch in the staff restaurant I found a pale and confused looking Alun sitting at his desk, staring into space and slowly shaking his head.

Sensing all was not well I managed to get him to describe his distress. He stated that we all knew our boss was a one-off and had distinctively annoying character traits but Alun now believed he was not of this world and possibly capable of time travel and/or teleportation and this may explain why our Board had been conned into employing him. I needed more proof which Alun provided.

"After I left you in the office still talking to him I walked straight up Grand Avenue and at the top I met him walking towards me from the opposite direction …. He couldn't have got there … I don't understand it!" The mystery was solved later that day when our resident genius told me that his twin brother was in Hove that day and had called for him for lunch. This was mildly reassuring to Alun when I told him

177

although he darkly speculated that he hoped the company would not be stupid enough to recruit the other twin.

Having been established with the title of Business Planning we had to convince the new directorates that there was some merit in having us 'internal outsiders' help or interfere, depending on your perspective. It is said that business planning is as much an art as a science and I agree with this. Some of the process is about a realistic assessment of where the business is currently before you can develop a vision or ambition of where it can be taken and what can be achieved. Along with all the fine words there is a need for hard data and often this is deftly hidden from 'outsiders' to support a story. One case in point was to help the operations director gain a better understanding of variations in profitability between his four divisions. Some analysis revealed that the least profitable division was winning high turnover from competitive bids with major construction projects but lower profitability margins whilst another division, less successful in winning contracts had redeployed much of their workforce on internal work such as rewiring their own offices which due to some historical practice was charged out at a guaranteed mark up, inflating profits. We painted a stark picture suggesting that division could become more profitable if they dispensed with the services of their marketing team as they clearly weren't winning contracts. Often it was not popular work as 'home truths' can be painful. We also help draw up and review plans for the company's retail division where it was becoming apparent that the scale of the operation was making it difficult to compete with the much larger national competitors.

Around this time I experienced my fortieth birthday which I had planned to be low key but unbeknown to me had been planned by my wife and work colleagues as a grand surprise garden party.

I was kept out of the way by being asked to take and collect a neighbour's daughter from some Saturday activity whilst food was brought in wheel barrows from storage at neighbours and a marquee was erected and by the time I arrived home the field part of our garden contained dozens of cars and some 140 friends were in hiding behind the hedge. It was a great success once I had got over the shock and lovely to see old friends and colleagues from near and far and definitely a great example of my wife's organisational abilities and our friends powers of discretion.

Gradually there was a move to integrate the planning function into the operating divisions and I like to think we had helped with a transfer of knowledge and established the discipline of business planning in the group.
My department was rebranded as Business Development with more emphasis on new unregulated business ventures and the first of these was an overseas consultancy joint venture. The intention was for the company to explore and develop business opportunities outside our core energy business but to use our existing skills in these new markets. The objective was to increase the groups profitability by adding unregulated profits to our existing regulated energy earnings.

The difficulties with my manager didn't improve. There was a classic case where we had been approached by ESB the Irish state owned company with the option of setting up a joint venture consultancy to access the international aid market. The two companies had good experience of working together on contracts associated with the Channel Tunnel project. ESB had been successfully carrying out assignments all around the world and were looking to JV with a UK electricity company which would allow access to contracts funded by Overseas Development Agency (ODA). Unfortunately, the initial meeting in

Dublin had not gone well and the accusation was that my manager had insulted them with his 'private enterprise expertise,' and they were quoted as saying if this was the sort of managers we had then a JV was out of the question. There was still an appetite for exploring the opportunity by our board so I was tasked with diplomatically recovering our reputation. After a phone call to Dublin I was asked if I could met with them soon in London at the offices of the ODA and give some assurances to the person there responsible for electricity contracts that we were serious in working together but cautioned that this person, a Dr Jones had been difficult to meet with.

So I felt I was on trial to prove something and placed a call to Dr Jones. He was initially frosty but agreed a meeting some weeks ahead but before I finished the call I asked him if he knew an old school friend of mine from Swansea, Jack Jones who also worked at the ODA. "How do you know Jack?" He asked.

I explained he was my first school friend from the age of four and we still see one another occasionally.

His attitude was transformed -

" I regularly have lunch with Jack - we call him Jones the Disaster as he runs the Emergency Aid desk for disaster recovery after earthquakes etc. Come in early before our meeting and we three welsh refugees can have coffee together." He then put me on hold and established Jack was there all week, subject to no new disasters and suggested we meet later the same week.

The ESB party were very impressed with the speed with which I had arranged the meeting and even more pleased when I explained the Welsh connection. They said that was closer to how things were done in Dublin and so later that week they're ready met with a positive reception at the ODA when they arrived and found me reminiscing and drinking coffee with the 'Jones Boys.'

The joint venture took several trips to Dublin to set up and on each occasion my new Irish colleagues looked after me very hospitably as well as any colleagues I had brought with me to later finalise the JV. A car collected me from the airport, I was put up in the Shelbourne Hotel in the city centre and enjoyed some pleasant business suppers. One time I was asked if I liked music and was told there was a piano recital in the City University that they would take me to, I must have been unconvincing in my enthusiasm as they said that I shouldn't worry as it was mostly chatting and drinking interspersed with short spells of music and would be followed by dinner out.

The JV was a success winning contracts around the world including Thailand, the Baltic states, some work in the Caribbean and South Africa. Typically, having set it up, the furthest I got from home was Dublin but it was very popular with the staff deployed on these contracts.

The staffing of my department was added to through the recruitment of an accountant with business development experience in the world of mergers and acquisitions in the City.

Arthur was a welcome addition to the group bringing real world business development experience and greater credibility in financial appraisals when being challenged by the finance director, (who always wanted his own accountants to check the finances in our proposals.) The finances must have impressed the FD as a few moths later he offered Arthur a position in the finance directorate; to my relief he turned the offer down.

I remember the personnel department amusing me by telling me they thought that Arthur was an old fashioned name. My reply with an arched eye brow suggested they check their records of a certain Geoffrey A. Dendle led to an embarrassed apology! This was also a time of some unease with the personnel department who had commissioned consultants to appraise jobs in the department for promotion to a new senior management group where

contracts would be offered with enhanced benefits such as share options, an improved car scheme as well as a salary increase. Three of my assistant managers were due to be assessed and having gone through the process myself the previous year I knew there was merit in preparation. To further complicate matters we were notified that there would be just one candidate interviewed and the result applied to all three positions. Of the three candidates two were graduates, one with only industry experience, the other with external business development experience. In the event the candidate with an accountancy qualification and mergers experience as well as an MBA was concluded as the strongest option and after a few hours of joint preparation the interview was successful with all three subsequently promoted.
A happy couple of years of assessing and developing business opportunities followed before an inevitable company restructuring was to throw all the balls up into the air again. Before that was to happen some more of those business ventures are described below.

Engaging in corporate 'jibber jabber!'

SOUTHERN gas

The next large scale business development that I was involved in was a gas business to take advantage of the newly deregulated gas market in the UK.

This was 90's Britain with new phone companies competing for business, gas companies offering electricity and new companies able to sell gas through the BG network. We were approached by a UK arm of a US utility who were looking for regional partners to market gas supples in competition with BG.

They were looking for business partners with proven experience of billing and customer management and we were an obvious choice.

An American utility had set up a UK trading subsidiary to buy gas supplies here and were looking to set up a number of joint venture companies with regional electricity companies who after recent legislative changes in the energy market here could be licences to sell gas to customers. A preliminary presentation had been made to our board of directors who concluded that it was worth exploring further. As the company's business development manager I was tasked with doing this. It was one of my initially most uncomfortable experiences as, somewhat ironically considering the nature of the business, I felt I was coming to this cold.

I didn't have much time to prepare as the meeting had even arranged to take place a few days after the presentation to the Board. I knew that there was a relatively new business analyst in another part of our organisation who had joined us from the oil and gas industry and a friend who worked with him suggested a chat with John could be useful. He was happy to help and I learned a few new terms used in the industry such as 'take or pay' contracts but still felt relatively unprepared for the next day's meeting.

The offices were a short walk from London's Victoria station and unbeknown to me at the time my journey could have taken a very nasty turn. During the walk I heard a distant muffled, distant thud. Later in the day I heard through the news broadcast that IRA terrorists had exploded a bomb on the station concourse with one fatality and dozens of injured.

Despite this narrow escape for me, which I only learned about later, the day went well as my tactic of admitting great ignorance about many important aspects of the gas business allowed my prospective business partners to patiently explain the process. I was starting to realise that my position was one that had been accurately described to me some time earlier as 'a Gatekeeper.'

For business proposals this meant that prospective partners needed to both give me a sound enough understanding and then convince me that there was merit in the company appraising it further. In a sense I was the gateway to potential approval by the Board. The gas company was an early success and our development team handed it over to operational staff. Other opportunities were appraised, some discarded and some pursued. I recall trying to convince my Board that the mobile telephony market growth projections that we had seen were realistic and being told that it would be unlikely that mobile phone ownership would ever become universal. 'What sort of people would let their children have phone accounts?' Funny in hindsight.

The situation with the manager was all a bit embarrassing as well as irritating but fortunately the irritation wasn't long lived and after less than two years he parted ways with the company by mutual agreement. One of the most irritating things about him was a habit of referring to himself in the third person which I personally found bizarre and suggested an underlying psychological problem. When he left I had already been promoted onto a senior management personal contract and its perhaps telling that his position wasn't filled.

It was time again for a company restructuring and this time it would include devolving many of the head office corporate functions out to the business units with a new, slimmed down head office to be established on a new site. In organisations a powerful reinforcement of change is to make people uncomfortable. This was certainly the case with this move as the head office with its population of several hundred had been in the five storey Victorian seafront building since nationalisation in 1948 and there were a few staff who probably began their careers there not long after. It was declared that the company would be embracing the current fashion for a core corporate function head office of essential functions that sat outside the operational activities or needed to be near the board of Directors. These were declared as corporate group finance, legal, shareholding, pensions, directors support and group strategy and regulation. There was a suggestion that the new head office should be only some 50 people but the prestige of being at the centre of things was tempered for most by the announcement that the new offices would be some twenty miles inland near Crawley, an anonymous new town and rather different from Brighton and Hove. One announcement stated that our building in Hove was no longer fit for purpose for modern businesses use, so it was with some sense of irony that it was sold to Brighton and Hove council to use as their offices. Personally, it made limited difference to me as I lived out to the north east from Brighton and had a similar commute to the new offices to the west of me. The main difference was the new role. The new structure had no place for my director who took early retirement but around this time I was asked by the new chief executive who I had already completed some work for both in business planning and the establishment of our gas company to undertake a short term project on his behalf.

Business Link Work

185

As a large company in the south east of England there was pressure to be involved in regional initiatives and one of these current ones was the TEC (Training and Enterprise Councils) and Business Link. From what I was told our CEO sat on the managing board for the Sussex TEC and had been critical of the piecemeal approach to strategy as well as the confusion of service provision by these two and the regional Chambers of commerce, As a solution he offered practical support in the form of two of his senior managers to fact find and publish recommendations in reports. Our outgoing Personnel director Chris, was one, I was the other although I was reassured it was not an exit route.

The CEO gave us a short briefing and explained the main objective was to get these agencies to work together and that an independent report may help to reveal the shortcomings of the present arrangements. My report was to cover what the various agencies could do to better cooperate in a unified economic strategy for Sussex whilst the other report was to look at improving skills and training. The initiative was to be launched at a large event in Brighton later that month. I gathered together as much relevant material as I could and together with some research from economic and business data we held put together a short presentation on the strengths and weaknesses of the county and covered the agencies engaged in development with a call to them to become engaged in the study and report. I tried to strike a balance between complimenting some achievements and provocation for more and better actions. The event turned out to be larger than I expected and it was the first time I had spoken in front of over five hundred people (unless you count my radio experience and believe BBC audience data - but at least I couldn't see that audience!)

There were a number of other topics presented at the event and judging by the conversations at coffee and afterwards much of the audience knew one another whereas Chris and myself were unknowns but represented an important player and employer in the area and all the more influential since privatisation. Our presentations were politely received although I worried that there could be an element of 'what do these two bozos know about this!' Afterwards a few people came up to us and asked to be involved and it was reassuring that some of them represented organisations that the CEO had suggested needed to be involved.

The next stage was to call together a working group of these representatives and follow up with any representations that were missing. At the first meeting there were over a dozen people, a mixture of economic development agencies such as the TEC, Chamber of Commerce etc as well as the two county councils of East and West Sussex, and some from unitary authorities such as Brighton, and Sussex university. There was also a cross section of business representatives from various sectors including one of the bank's senior managers. At the first meeting we concentrated on drawing up the terms of reference, scope, methodology and timescale as well os the objectives. They were typed up and faxed out to the members and copied to the TEC board members. Within hours I seemed to have made a powerful enemy as the next morning my phone rang and it was the chief executive of East Sussex council.

"These minutes and terms of reference have been sent out before I had a chance to agree them!"

I pointed out that as he wasn't at the meeting it was difficult to see how he could accurately agree them and I assumed his representative on the group had been able to speak for their organisation but if not then could he nominate someone who could or perhaps attend himself.

"Has you CEO agreed this?"

Again I politely explained that he had been sent a copy the same time as everyone else but had delegated the project to me.

He clearly wasn't happy.

By the time I got to see my CEO he had already had a phone call which he was laughing about having apparently enjoyed giving a lecture on speed and delegation in the private sector to the council leader. "Just keep on doing what you are doing - this whole area needs waking up if they are to achieve anything."

The next few weeks I visited all the group members and some other places recommended including an early cyber cafe facility, tourism offices and other workplaces. It shows how times have changed when it was thought that in the mid 1990's people needed to go to a specific location outside their home to get internet access!

I arranged the first meeting for the two county directors of education to compare issues which to my amazement had never happened before for them. The businesses were frank in their criticism of structural weaknesses in the economy. Their examples included poor east west transport communications; difficulties in declining seaside towns; the reliance on certain dominant sectors and the competition for labour with London. It was an interesting exercise and although we had researched aspects of the local economy for our own business plans I learnt more about the area from the different perspectives.

Chris compared notes with me on his findings on training and skills which complemented my own information and I passed on my findings.

While I found the exercise interesting and it took me outside my own environment for a while and also gave me a better perspective of the challenges faced by businesses and organisations in the county I lived in I am afraid it also developed in my a healthy cynicism when I hear that a report has been commissioned as often you worry post-publication that they just get filed away on shelves. Earlier in my career I had helped promote the company's sponsorship of an Innovation Centre on the campus at Sussex university to incubate start up companies for post-graduates with business ideas. Shared facilities such as legal services, finance advice and office bureaus were provided. I felt that more such practical initiatives were needed to build on any strategy documents.

Strategy and Regulation Group

As with many things you are not always aware that some of your actions or things you get involved with will have benefits to be realised later. The business development and planning work had raised my profile after the success of the ESB joint venture and the establishment of our first de-regulated gas business. One of the corporate functions to be part of the new slim-line head office was a 'think tank' to advise the CEO and it was christened the SRG, abbreviated from the mouthful of Strategy and Regulation group. It was to be headed senior manager at director level who reported to the CEO and would have eight or ten staff in a flat structure, a mix of senior managers and relatively recent graduates considered to be rising stars. I was pleased to be asked to join as one of the first recruits and reassured that there had been some recognition of some of my successes in business planning and development in setting up our international consultancy and gas businesses. What the new group would be doing was more uncertain but initially I needed to ensure that the other members of my now defunct business planning department were found new jobs and in a company undergoing a major reorganisation it may not be so easy. I felt a strong sense of responsibility in achieving this as I had personally recruited all of them and it wasn't either my fault or theirs that our directorate was disbanded. In the event the relatively high profile of our group and the contribution made by the whole team in our successes helped the first three of the team find new interesting positions and the fourth member was selected to join me in the new strategy group.

The formation of this new group was followed by the move to the new slimmer corporate head office from the large extended Victorian seafront building to a new build anonymous three story box style building on a business park in mid-Sussex outside Crawley. For shopping and eating facilities it was a backward step but the company still retained an in-house staff restaurant which provided subsidised meals of good quality. The office was spacious and modern with most of the directors and senior managers either in open plan spaces or glass cubicles. The pleasant lunch time seafront walks could be replaced by walks in the adjacent Tilgate forest county park and the shopping centre of Crawley, whilst less interesting than Brighton shops, was a short drive away.

Before the move the group started work including advising the CEO on potential initiatives to increase efficiency in the company. For a couple of months two of us, myself and a younger senior manager, Steve, met weekly with the CEO to brainstorm ideas for initiatives. Some were dismissed out of hand others were selected for further development. It was a great opportunity to work at the very top of the company in a refreshing and open way. Two things resulted from this.

Firstly we were seen in the company as people with the ear of the CEO and to be wielding more influence than our previous positions suggested. This was confirmed when we discovered a colleague in one of the larger engineering divisions was experimenting with a flatter structure with a philosophy similar to the Japanese 'kaizen,' or continuous improvement philosophy with all his staff members encouraged to contribute their ideas. He was very enthusiastic about this and we suggested his approach needed to be heard and we put this to the CEO who agreed. It was arranged that Harry would present his initiative to the whole management group and he agreed somewhat reluctantly. It raised his profile and I believe it was a success but some of the more cynical managers of functions were for a time rather cautious in speaking to us in case they were called upon in the same way. Within the SRG there was also a little jealousy expressed that we had been given direct access, at least for a time, to the CEO and board as this was normally the role performed by our group head Tony.

It was an interesting time in a new environment with new people with different backgrounds. The work was varied often requiring assessment of the impact on the company of external changes whether of a competitive nature, legislative changes or government policy. I had experienced enough changes in my career to know that like everything, it would have a limited lifespan and I enjoyed the environment while I could.

Around this time one of those out of the blue opportunities came up and it demonstrates that past endeavours can later combine in unexpected ways. I was called into the chairman and told he had been asked by one of our advisor companies if we would be able to assist them on one of their consultancy projects. It was advising one of the state governments in India, specifically Orissa on the privatisation of their electricity company. The partner leading the project had returned to the London for family reasons and they needed a credible replacement. It was thought my experience establishing out own aid funded consultancy together with my role as privatisation manager here previously might be what they were looking for. It was explained to me that it was voluntary but in the meantime could I go to their head office in the city tomorrow morning to discuss it and a version of my CV experience had been prepared quickly by HR for me to show them!

It appeared that the company had some enthusiasm for this although I realised that the fees for a partners charges from a major consultancy would be a welcome sum to our fledgling consultancy business (and I wouldn't be seeing any of it.) Nevertheless I was flattered to be asked.

The next morning found me on the train to the city offices having discussed the offer at home and also hoping to get back to our offices for our staff xmas lunch which I was reluctant to miss.

The discussion seemed to go well but I was rather pushy with the suited representative in his large, luxurious office overlooking the river Thames. There were two reasons for this: the first was he seemed rather vague about the project details and I felt I wanted a lot more information so the meeting was protracted whilst he phoned people for answers to me questions and on several occasions left to office to get answers. The second reason was I could see as the morning went on the prospect of my anticipated lavish xmas lunch vanishing. I eventually rushed back to our office just in time for a belated xmas lunch during which the chairman with a big grin told me he had had two phone calls - one from the guy I had met to say he had been impressed and wanted to put forward my CV to the Indian government and a second call from his amused assistant with details of vaccinations required and a statement that he had been impressed with my capabilities as 'few people get our Head of Corporate Finance flustered and running around the office.' My chairman was amused and darkly said it was a good job I was better behaved on home ground.

In the event the client government told the consultancy that they wouldn't allow a substitute from another company and they had paid for a partner and expected to get one. Thankfully, this was before any vaccinations had been arranged so my six months in the sun was not to be.

My exit from the SRG came after we had been looking at cost cutting initiatives in the operating businesses and somewhere in this one of the many consultancy firms we used after privatisation suggested they could help the company undertake a major review of our purchasing and supply chain processes. I must have looked sufficiently underemployed or less incapable than alternative candidates so was asked by the board of directors to project manage the initiative. As with many paths in my career this area was relatively new to me; the company had professionally qualified buyers and purchasing professionals but a fresh approach apart from them was recommended. I knew from experience how this would be likely to go, at least initially. The task was for someone not from a supply chain background to work with our procurement professionals to develop their skills to source and buy products and services more effectively. It was certainly going to be a challenge. Like many specialists at work there is a form of tribalism and assumed mystery to shield activities from other colleagues who are not tribal members. I was certainly met with initial suspicion and accusations that as my background was in customer service and finance I would to be able to fully understand their processes and 'mysterious techniques.' I dealt with this by answering that I had pursued a number of varied roles in the group in my career and this was the latest. I explained that I was not after a long term career in purchasing but only leading a review at the request of our CEO and Board and that the greater degree of their cooperation would see the process over with sooner. Also my lack of particular purchasing expertise would supplemented by our consultant partner who had a past career as a national buyer for a large UK plc.

Whilst all of this is plausible to a neutral observer it did little to initially dispel suspicions that I may be after their jobs and wanted to become some elevated group purchasing manager. It was easy for me to protest against this as truthfully that was the last thing I had ambitions for.

The first thing I had to do was recruit a small team for the project and is often the way in established companies those employees who believe that they are secure in their current roles, (sometimes mistakenly as the next reorganisation is never far away!) are reluctant to join a temporary project team. I had no such fears believing that the skills required in projects and new roles are not only more marketable but also for me kept me more interested in work than I had been in established permanent roles. I was fortunate in finding a experienced manager who was an accountant from our payments function of the finance department and a younger member of staff studying for an MBA who was keen to extend his experience. Later we added another accountant who was seconded from internal audit and a legal secretary with good contracts experience.

The second task was to find a project office. The requirement for the project to work creatively with line managers led me to believe that a location away from the businesses or the corporate head office would benefit the creative process. Through a chance conversation with the company architect I discovered that he had a suitable space on a mezzanine floor in his own office that he had ambitions to improve by installing skylights. The offices were right in the centre of Brighton with dedicated parking and close to the Brighton pavilion. More attractively there were a wide range of eateries and cafes and pubs in walking distance. The building alterations were made in a very short and a few weeks later we moved in.

The consultant enjoyed her time challenging some of the dyed in the wool engineering brethren many of which found having their practices questioned by an outsider and a woman to present them with some discomfort. A lot of time in the initial weeks was occupied constructing a 'spend map' for the group highlighting spends on services and products with the same items subject to different contracts from a number of suppliers. When I made an initial presentation to the Board there was a lot of defensive justifications from the business managing directors over their own contracts while the disparities were scrutinised gleefully by the finance director and the CEO. Often excuses over prices were exposed with some smaller value contracts being at better prices than larger ones. The support from the Board going forward was very helpful in gaining access into the businesses and anticipated improvement and savings meant the initiative was given a high priority. On the advice of the consultants we started examining spend areas that experience told them would bring early gains.

One area was the leasing contracts for photocopiers which in the early days of intranets and emails was a significant expense for the group. We found that the group had a total photocopier population of over 150 with an annual expenditure to the suppliers in excess of £ 2 million. After some digging through the contract paperwork we were able to establish that significant monthly charges were being incurred for machines in unoccupied offices and depots. Including refunds for estimated charges, the cancellation of leases on machines no longer required totalled almost £500,000 with future annual savings of over £400K per annum. It was a good early win for the project and proved the value of thoroughly mapping spends.

Early on in the project there was a change in the consultants we were using and a new contract was let to a Supply chain specialist who had developed their skills originally at General Motors. They were more aggressive and confrontational than the first consultants and led to some stormy meetings within the company but first hand reports from clients at previous assignments confirmed that their ambitious claims of results were achievable.

Early on in the project it was agreed that we would run a one day event for our top hundred suppliers at a Brighton seafront hotel to launch the initiative and to explain that we were looking at collaborative ways of working with them to find mutual benefits in our supply chains. An important part of this was to be a frank exchange of feedback on how we were to do business with. On the day in a large conference room with some nervousness I outlined the project and the objectives for it to over a hundred members of our supplier companies. Later in the morning we recorded their feedback on us as a customer and a salutary experience it was as 'punches were not pulled!'

I was told that we were demanding as a customer in some cases to the point of arrogance, poor at forecasting demands, slow to pay and resistant to innovations. The only good news was that we were seen to be financially secure so slow payment was tolerated but the negative effect on that cash flow could often be passed on to us in pricing. On a positive note many of the delegates expressed enthusiasm to work with us on improvements including the more important and strategic suppliers such as the metering, cable and switchgear companies. It was clear that there was a lot of work to do but my first task was to convey the comments back to my Board. I was now scheduled to give monthly updates to the directors and after the good news of the savings on photocopiers the previous month my latest update after the feedback from our suppliers may get a different reception. Initially my report was met with some cynicism and reactions of 'well, they would say that wouldn't they,' but there was a realisation that many of the suppliers were interested in working with us to jointly reduce costs and streamline our processes. The next stage was to set up 'sourcing groups' to understand our purchases more fully and for this we would hold meetings where every link in the supply chain would be represented from specifiers to warehouse staff and users.

I guess the details are of limited interest to others but included such lessons as how suppliers delivered to us and that goods could be damaged if pallets were overloaded. Similarly, by being more transparent with switchgear suppliers over our planned maintenance programmes there were financial gains possible for both of us. It was hard work and eventually involved people from most corners of the organisation. The consultancy fees were expensive but the finance director said it was the best return on investment that the company had made that year.

An amusing encounter happened during the project when we were running some project workshops in the Brighton Metropole hotel on the seafront. Late on the final evening I was ordering a round of drinks at the bar for members of the project when I noticed two tall, slim men standing beside me and I recognised them as singer Jarvis Cocker and comedian Vic Reeves. Fortified by my own drinks and not ever fazed by so called celebrity I smiled at them and found myself saying 'Bob not with you -then,' referring to Vic's comedy partner Mr Mortimer. It was met with an almost curt response of 'not tonight,' before we parted to our prospective tables. When checking out the next morning I found that the band Pulp were checking out having played at the Brighton Conference centre next door the previous night but it was only later that I discovered the Bob and Jarvis connection. The day before the concert Jarvis had attended the Brit awards and had run on stage during Michael Jackson's concert performance surrounded by children (eek) and expressed his displeasure in the 'Christ like' stance by waving his clothed bottom at the self proclaimed 'king of pop.' He had been apprehended by a group of Jackson's security and Bob Mortimer had intervened calling on his legal training to release Jarvis (the king of Pulp?) from both the security and the police who were now involved. It seemed that the episode only just over 24 hours before was still raw and may have explained their response. In a world without smart phones and rolling news I was unaware of this recent trauma!

The project carried on for a few more months but it was time for me to do something different and I was approached to work on the preparations for the deregulation of the electricity market.

It was during this time that my company along with a number of the newly privatised RECs became targets for take overs by foreign utilities; many of them borrowing heavily to fund the purchase. These ownerships, in some cases, didn't last long as a misunderstanding of the regulated UK market led to over optimistic expectations of profits from these deals.

1998 Competitive Market

Unsurprisingly, during the decades of my career there were a large number of changes, some self generated, some imposed by legislative initiatives. The latest of these was the further de-regulation of the electricity market; this time to extend the choice of suppliers to domestic and small business customers. It was a logical change to allow electricity customers the freedom of choice they enjoyed when buying most other goods and services.

It sounds a simple enough change but in an industry that was extensively computerised with different systems with no thought given to compatibility with those used by other suppliers it was not a simple matter. Much of the work centred around allowing customer data to be transferred to the new supplier's systems and all of this was to be accomplished in an ambitious timescale of less than two years. Various project teams were in place when I switched roles from managing the supply chain project to a project director of several project teams in the Customer business. The project was supported by external consultants as well as staff from within the business including some recently retired staff re-employed on contract and couldn't believe their luck being paid a salary as well as their pensions. The work was high pressure but creative but due to the high costs being incurred was subject to intense review with many regular progress and monitoring meetings. I think it was the time in my career when the majority of my time was spent in meetings reporting progress or more often explaining the reasons for the lack of it rather than actually working on progressing the project. I was fortunate to have a good team of people working with me and over the months the teams grew as the deadlines for going live came nearer. I had some prior experience when we entered the competitive gas business a few years earlier and was able to draw on lessons learnt there, in particular the need for robust testing and piloting. We set up what became known as the 'model office' to test customer exchange and to my shame I always had a mental picture of an office made of Lego populated with little Lego figures. Wisely, I kept this image to myself.

Coming into a business as a member of the senior management team but being a project manager rather than a line manager brought a new set of problems. The business was just recovering from the launch of a large IT project central to the business of customer management and there was a certain amount of 'project weariness' as well as a desire to get back to business as usual. I also knew that as the project developed we would need to beg, borrow and steal additional members of staff from within the business. Management meetings were weekly at 8 a.m. on Monday mornings and conducted around a large table in conference room and although an extra chair was made available for me it was clear that the managers sat in the same positions and had been doing so for the last couple of years. I amused myself by sitting in a different position each week and ignored their protests,(like Sheldon in the Big Bang Theory,) that I was occupying 'their spot!' I used the lesson of this a few weeks later when describing the scale and extent of the change that market-deregulation would bring both to the business and the whole industry as rather more uncomfortable and radical than moving to a new chair!

The impact of the project became more obvious after a couple of months as more staff were co-opted onto the project and my project team expanded from a handful to dozens in a number of locations. Regular work stream meetings were held with different parts of the business to explain the likely impact that the new open domestic energy market would have for them.

There was added pressure to the programme by the decision to allow suppliers to enter the competitive market in waves and there was thought to be a certain amount of quodos to be gained by being one of the four or five companies in the first wave so this became an objective for the company. The job became one of managing expectations as well as driving progress. I had a good team to work with and as the deadlines were reached and met more staff were deployed onto the projects. At a critical point in the project it was decided, (not by me !!), that it would be useful for a party of representatives from our American owners to get a first hand update on the progress of the project. This wasn't the best thing to happen as the Chairman selected me to be 'shadowed' by the three visitors for the week and I could explain the complexities of the deregulation programme. The three senior staff from the Texan owners were polite and attentive and we got on well although there was a dawning realisation that due to a number of factors, geography, regulatory and social amongst others, we faced different challenges this side of the Atlantic whilst superficially providing similar services. Trish, Don and John were good company and although the working week was busy as we neared some critical programme deadlines there was a little time for socialising with a couple of suppers together. None of them had visited Europe before so I asked them if they had any must-do's. They had a spare day in London before they left so that might fix their historic needs but they also asked to see a castle or at least an old house. To meet this I drove them past the Brighton Pavilion on our way up to see the model office in Croydon where we were in the latter stages of system testing for customer migrations due to go live shortly.

They were surprised to hear that the Pavilion only dated back the early nineteenth century having been completed in 1823 and I said that my house was older than that as at the time we lived in a tile hung beamed cottage on the High Weald borders of Kent and Sussex and had dated the house pre 1760 in the county records office. On the way back from Croydon we detoured home for tea and cakes and the three visitors took photos of the beamed ceilings, flagstone floor and ingle nook fireplaces, as well as our large friendly Irish Wolfhound who was always pleased to welcome visitors particularly if cake was on offer and he lent a medieval aspect to the visit to the house. Anxious to enhance their stay I was guilty of telling a white lie, appropriately about the white cliffs of Dover. We were returning to Brighton after a tedious day of meetings when one of them asked me whether the white cliffs of Dover were really white and how far away they were from where we were. A short detour to Rottingdean allowed them to get out and take photos of the Sussex Severn Sister cliffs which, not wishing to spoil their joy, I assured them were the famous white cliffs of Dover. The next day I had to swear colleagues in the office to secrecy so that for that day the Dover cliffs could be easily glimpsed from Brighton. The visitors were pleased and maybe honesty isn't always the best policy.

 My time with the visitors had an unexpected bonus that I am not entirely sure was coincidental. The company was dabbling with a style of macho management popular in the 1990's and one particular keen exponent was bullying staff in the Customer directorate having been given a free hand by the new CEO, personally, I thought against better judgement, as a temporary change manager. I had already had a couple of run ins with him and had, to date successfully confused him with detailed papers and complex explanations about the national de-regulation project to the extend that he threatened 'to return to deal with me when he had sorted out the other managers in the business. I seem to remember saying that I was confident that my career in the company would outlast him and hoped this was true and I would find a way to 'fix him.' The business was not happy during this time and it didn't help me with my own change programme. When the American colleagues were with me and reviewing the progress of the de-regulation project it was clear to them as experienced professionals that there was some underlying issue and they asked if this atmosphere of fear was caused by my project. I denied this and decided they should meet the cause of the distress so I invited this manager who we will call Paul to meet them to explain his management style.

It couldn't have gone better; he was on his worst behaviour, offensive, swearing, chauvinistic, critical of all and sundry, particularly of utility professionals, ignoring the fact that he was talking to an audience of those and to his cost, professionals who had the ear of both our Board and that of our owners. When he brusquely announced that he had spent enough of his time with us and he had 'people to sort out' and left, I only needed to raise my eyebrows. Within a matter of weeks Paul was dismissed and I wonder whether there had been a deliberate tactic of exposing him through me to the influential visitors; I can't prove it but the CEO came to tell me face to face that he was going. I made the most of it by going to a Paul's office before he left, to say goodbye. It was very satisfying for me; less so for him as in his barely suppressed anger he pulled the handle off the mug he was holding and nearly scalded himself with hot coffee. Sometimes revenge doesn't have to be served cold!

I absorbed a number of lessons through my time managing projects and I mention a few here:-

Keep an eye on the ultimate goal or overall objective; Progress will not be smooth;

Celebrate victories along the way;

Encourage team members to expose obstacles early and review mistakes or delays positively;

Keep an 'open door policy' for team members to download fears or mistakes;

Develop solutions en route as most projects are new territories without prescribed solutions;

Don't be afraid to flag problems or delays early to the sponsor or managing board - an early small delay will be more palatable than a hidden bigger one later and if more resources are required document the request;

Review progress regularly with project milestones and targets;

And sometimes you have to 'play the long game,' but when revenge comes it can be all the sweeter.

Business Separation

After the market opened for domestic customers the regulator for the industry turned their attention to the issue of cross-subsidy i.e. whether companies who both supplied and distributed electricity were subsidising their supply businesses from the network business. Companies were asked to demonstrate that the business costs were being fairly allocated in their businesses.

I was asked to work on the response to this and to do so needed to collect cost data to show fair allocations. It wasn't the most interesting of projects and involved much of my time convincing members of the company's financial fraternity to stop mucking about with their endless financial forecasts and urgently provide me with some real and credible cost analyses. In the end I temporarily recruited one of their number onto the team and she collected much of the data for us. The regulator had ambitions to completely separate ownership of the businesses but this wasn't a shared ambition by my company. In the event some kind of compromise was achieved via more visible financial reporting. I think my Board was satisfied with the outcompete for us so I chalked it up as another successfully completed project and looked around for something else to do.

E-commerce strategy

I seemed to have demonstrated to my Board an expertise in taking on projects in new areas and believe this was down to a mixture of confidence, an enthusiasm for new challenges and maybe a dose of naivety. In any event I now enjoyed a senior position in the company without any permanent staff responsibilities, or a fixed role and a direct report to the Chief executive who I enjoyed a good working relationship with. This was met by some of my contemporaries and management equals with a mixture of envy for my apparent lack of visible responsibilities and freedom and dire warnings about the dangers of not having 'a real job.' These were usually given whilst moaning about their workload, their difficult staff and many other problems, real or imagined.

The next new challenge was to develop for the Board an e-commerce strategy and given that this was early in the 21st century when companies had already spend huge sums of money to avoid the real or imagined problems that their IT departments had warned them about Y2K computer problems there was a certain cynicism abroad about large spends by IT departments. Ours was no exception having creating a Y2K task force of employees and consultants to examine our IT systems for Y2K compliance. In spite or perhaps because of all this effort planes did not drop out of the sky, power networks continued to operate and cash machines continued to spout money. There was an understandable reluctance on the part of the IT department to have the e-commerce strategy authored by someone outside the IT department and I had some fun by both saying it wasn't my choice but I was the one selected by the Board so their 'shopping lists' needed to be convincing to me. I am sure that my other statement that I had worked in their department some twenty years before so had a strong insight into their work also did much to 'wind them up,' particularly amongst those who had

207

been there at that time and would have heard me saying that the atmosphere and work pressure there was much less than in the rest of the company. I initially brought myself up to speed on the current state of e-commerce by some desk study and calling in favours from some external sources and Michael Hartz who I had worked with on the sourcing project was particularly helpful directing me to some white papers on key subjects. I then compared some of these opportunities to our own business processes that I had knowledge of to identify likely areas for development. I felt I was then ready for some preliminary discussions with our IT folk. The dialogue was not easy and I needed to be quite forceful to convince them that I was the one who would be putting proposals for these initiatives to the Board of directors and they would need to work with me to get a hearing for any of their projects in this area. Looking back from today it is hard to realise how some of the proposals some twenty plus years ago were viewed with cynicism. These included web based recruitment processes, self-service applications for customers, ebilling and other applications I have since forgotten. The difficulty at that time was that no one had foreseen how the internet and connected devices would spread to become a part of everyday life for most people and this slowed investment in e-commerce applications for organisations that were often 'conservative' in their vision.

My strategy was well received and in time the majority of the proposals were adopted but I began to wonder whether my time with the company was coming to an end.

SEEDA

The reason for this was a conversation I had with the CEO who now numbered me among his direct reports in the small corporate head office. He explained that the company chairman was a board member of the regional development agency for the south east of England, SEEDA and had offered some support to the organisation in the form of a secondment. It had been remembered that I had worked on regional regeneration strategy some years back with a previous regional organisation, the Sussex TEC and it was felt that I had some useful experience to offer. At the time the company was offering some early retirement packages to senior managers who had served the thirty years required for full pension entitlement and I wondered whether this was the precursor to a retirement offer. John's protestations that this wasn't the case were only partially convincing but in the event I thought it would be a useful way of making new business contacts in the area that could help me in retirement as it would be likely that I would be looking for some part time work or consultancy assignments.

So having agreed to the secondment I found myself in a modern office in Guildford having endured a commute across the Home Counties that added an extra hour each way to my daily journey. East - west travel across Sussex and Surrey is tortuous at the best of times but the peak hours and extensive roadworks along the route that year only added to the time. The fact that the extra fuel was being paid for and the mileage was in my beloved company Alfa Romeo only helped a bit. Once I had established myself there by a combination of quickly arranging meetings elsewhere, it was quicker to get to central London! I did all I could to reduce time spent at the SEEDA offices in Guildford.

This even included having an extra phone line and modem installed at home and trialling the now ubiquitous WFH (working from home,) that in the 1990's seemed more revolutionary.

The work was made slightly more enjoyable by the company of another temporary employee, who amongst the permanent career civil servants was a breath of fresh air. The proposed temporary roles for David and myself were to identify the major companies in the major business sectors in the area covered by the agency and to raise their awareness of SEEDA and to discuss any services that could be offered to them.

One benefit of the placement was to provide me with another uniquely new experience, lunch in a London gentlemen's club.
The club in question was the Savile Club in Mayfair, apparently established by a group of writers in 1868. I fully expected it would be like the Drones club frequented by Bertie Wooster and it was!
I had taken the precaution of coming by train and having a lift to the station as I had been warned that the club had a good cellar so after the planned morning meeting in the city, the purpose and venue now lost to me, we were dropped by cab at the club door.
It lived up to my preconceptions. David was greeted by name by the uniformed doorman who took our coats and briefcases, (this was pre-rucksacks to work days!) I followed my guide down the tiled hallway, resplendent with wood panelling and large crystal chandeliers. He showed me the first room a comfortable, low lit bar room, empty at present but lavishly furnished and said we would first of all go to the library. This was upstairs but at the door David indicated we should be quiet by putting a finger to his lips before slowly and quietly opening the door. Within was a large room, each wall lined with floor to ceiling bookcases. Scattered around the room were a number of high backed, leather chesterfield style armchairs and scattered in a number of them were besuited gentlemen, some with newspapers open in their laps and others with books discarded on low tables or arms of their chairs. All of them were soundly asleep - some quietly, others contentedly snoring. We quietly left and

closed the door behind us - "the breakfast crowd !"
David said with a smile - "but don't worry the
lunchtime bell will wake them up for refreshments."
I wondered how popular the library must be after a
hearty Club lunch.
Before lunch we went down to the club bar that was a
bit busier and those present were more, well present,
than the occupants of the library. Several rounds of
pre-lunch drinks were drunk with David introducing
me to a number of other jovial, (and wide awake club
members) and it was soon time to go to the dining
room for lunch. I wasn't shown a menu and it seemed
that that day there was a set lunch. The first course
arrived quickly which was a hearty soup that I
reckoned was oxtail and was accompanied by large
warm bread rolls. This was followed by a roast beef
dinner with all the trimmings such as sprouts and
parsnips with horseradish sauce etc. Generous
helpings of wine were served and I noticed that
several of the 'refreshed' occupants of the library had
made it to the dining room presumably either having
been roused by the bell or lured by the wafting roast
flavours.
Already rather full, the sweet course arrived which
was a large helping of treacle sponge with custard!
Suddenly an afternoon in an armchair dozing in the
library seemed a very appealing prospect. Instead,
coffee back in the bar with the more hardened
members adding liqueurs. I was glad that our London
meeting had been before lunch and also realised why
Bertie Wooster and his fellow Drones club members
were unemployable.

The secondment itself was not a wholly satisfying
experience. I had been told that our chairman during
his membership of their managing board had been
critical of some of the organisation's operation and to
some extent it's purpose and usefulness. I had gained
the impression that he wanted one of his people
'inside' to either confirm his suspicions or to convince

211

him that it may be worth him devoting more time and energy to his commitment if it would be seen as beneficial to our own organisation.

The work included visiting companies so it was enlightening to see the scale of successful pharmaceutical laboratories and see wind turbines being manufactured on the Isle of Wight and I met some interesting people during the secondment and learned a little more about 'government Enterprise assistance'. But my conclusion was that businesses and industries were likely to come to the south east anyway and it seemed an unnecessary distraction for our company to have a more extensive role with the organisation and it seemed that my chairman had privately come to a similar conclusion and was just looking for confirmation of this.

As an interesting aside a few years later the Regional development agencies were abolished by the government to be replaced by LEPs!

Return to Corporate Life

On my return to head office one of the themes of the 1990's was affecting the company. A few years before Seeboard had been bought up by an American electricity company CSW, based in Houston, Texas. We were not the only UK utility to be acquired in this way and foreign investors seemed keen to take shares in the deregulated environment here. Within a couple of years CSW were taken over by a larger US company, AEP (American Electric Power) based in Columbus, Ohio. Both owners were relatively 'arms length' in their management and for a while were content to collect their dividends apart from occasional visits of their senior staff, (which some cynics noticed often coincided with Wimbledon fortnight, Cowes week or Royal Ascot.) The honeymoon was short lived as AEP were also part-owners of Yorkshire Electricity plc, and there was a serious proposal of a merger and creation of a single corporate head office and board of directors. This idea was encouraged by the apparent short distance on a map, at least to American eyes unfamiliar with the UK's congested transport system and used to free flowing US freeways. This view was confirmed by one visit to us in the morning and a proposed quick drive from Sussex to Leeds after a leisurely lunch as it 'didn't look far on the map!' Our 2.30 pm phone call to colleagues in Leeds suggested they might be in for a late night.

Despite this I was involved for several months with others in an exercise making cost comparisons and efficiency reviews between the two companies. I don't know whether their tortuous journey round the M25 and up the motorway to Leeds played a part but it was announced that our American friends were to put Seeboard up for sale and planned to exit the UK energy market.

Company sale

My next role was a long way from the day I had sat in the reception area in York House, Folkestone and causing some consternation with my unexpected arrival. The US owners of the company were putting us up for sale and it seemed that I was to have a central role in this process. The initial task was editing and finalising the Prospectus for the company which is in effect a sales brochure. An earlier draft had been prepared but it needed extending, updating and checking for accuracy. A merchant bank had been appointed to work on the sale and meetings began with them, representatives of our corporate lawyers as well as Seeboard staff. I remember one meeting in the city when on looking out of the window many floors up down to a curious shaped construction site below. At the time I didn't know that I was looking at the foundations of the office block later christened 'the Gherkin' and eventually one of the iconic new buildings in London.

Once the prospectus was finalised there was a discussion over responsibilities during the sale process itself and my role in the prospectus compilation led to a new responsibility during the sale. The bank advisors explained that it was vital that questions raised by the approved bidders needed a consistent response and would need recording and the responses would need to be managed in the company, directed speedily to the right people and the answers approved before returning. It sounded like a load of work and quite a responsibility but the bitter pill of it was that it could turn out to be a kind of crowning glory in my career.

When I had agreed earlier to the role in the sale in completing the prospectus I had indicated to the CEO that I was now at the point in my career that early retirement would be my favoured option and there had been a verbal understanding that after the sale this could be discussed and looked on favourably. Tensions emerged during the sale process as the merchant bank were working on behalf of our parent company but needed extensive input and cooperation from us, possibly the victims in the piece, and our role might be seen as that of turkeys voting for xmas!

There was particular suspicion from the AEP board that emerged once the short list of confirmed bidders was announced and as the appointed contact for handling questions from the bidders I was placed in the invidious position of being told not to reveal to my own directors the identities of the potential new owners. In practical terms this was solved during a series of 'guessing games,' where my response using eyebrows and the fact we had been working together for so long that they were informed without me actually betraying any confidences made to our remote owners.

A room in the corporate head office had been set aside as a 'data room' with the documents there availed to pre scheduled scrutiny by bidders but more frequently used by us to check our approved replies to

214

bidders questions received by email and circulated via our intranet for reply.

Over a period of a couple of months several thousand questions were received and replied to. The hours were long and stressful through the pressure with occasional meetings with lawyers and bankers. At the height of activity there were daily conference calls with the owners in Ohio, normally scheduled for 6 or 7 p.m. for their convenience. It was occasionally satisfying to find that one of the bidders would resend a question that I had already sent them an answer for which made for a quick turnaround and gave me some private satisfaction that they may be less well organised than we were. Eventually a deal was struck with a sale price of some one and a half billion pounds! Although much of the process had been handled via emails there was a requirement to finalise the deal on paper so that one autumn morning I found myself on the train to an office near Trafalgar Square carrying a briefcase with a set of final documents for signature by our owners UK representatives and those lawyers acting for the buyers. The process itself was quite low key and comprised a couple of signatures and a couple of phone calls confirming the transfer of funds. It was all rather an anti-climax but as I carried my now empty brief case back to the station I contemplated how far this day was from me arriving unexpectedly to the small Seeboard office in Folkestone over thirty years before.

Differences in work

In my first full time job the telephone, handwriting converted to typed documents and photocopiers were the technologies employed. There were mains operated electronic calculators and some letters or memos were dictated onto tape and transcribed by typists or secretaries listening via headsets. My company of some 9000 people apparently owned and operated two computers, one mainframe in its own controlled air conditioned environment and communicated with by a small band of specialist, the other was some kind of mini computer for rudimentary mathematical models. Output from both was on paper printed at the computer or nearby.

My working life saw the transition from that world to on-line terminals, desk top pc's, desk top publishing, pagers, mobiles, emails and intranets and migration of operations onto the internet as well as other developments which continue today with Zoom and smart phone apps for everything.

My first company mobile phone was only mobile in the sense it was attached to my car! On one of my later projects in the late 1990's to avoid a journey of almost two hours to an office the other side of the Home Counties with poor road connections east to west and heavy traffic. To work remotely for even a couple of days a week meant installing a separate phone line, a slow dial up modem for the laptop and a fax machine and it was still frustrating to connect to the company's intranet. Nowadays communication is instant, seamless but inescapable. It's very different but has also served to blur the boundaries between home and work with the attendant reassures that can bring.

I have mentioned earlier the insidious influence of American influences into many aspects of British life and the impact of this was certainly felt during my working life.

One particular area is business jargon and although I have described my industry's love of acronyms, generally the meanings once expanded become clear but since the late 1980's and into the 21st century some terms used defy understanding. I believe as well we have gone through some changes influenced by social trends in society at large. Certainly the business environment post de-regulation and the Big Bang used very aggressive sounding, macho style terms and was about 'Quick wins', leading edge, win-wins, silos, outflanking competitors, campaigns, end-game and many other militaristic sounding terms. Recent years have hopefully seen a softening of attitudes and a recognition of emotional intelligence and this may have more than something to do with the effect of greater number of women in the workplace in more senior positions of power, (I mean, influence) no more so than in the media.

Certainly, this is a welcome trend and the recognition of bullying in the workplace as unacceptable is only one example.

This week I read a news article that the prestigious Harvard Business school are running very popular classes on 'Leadership and Happiness,' unthinkable in earlier times.

Another major difference that has occurred over the span of my thirty year plus career is that at the beginning of my career it would not have been that unusual for people to begin and end their careers in the same organisation. Although the working environment changed extensively as well as the ownership I essentially had my whole career with the same organisation and for someone starting theirs in more recent years, that is becoming much more unlikely.

I am also aware that part of my career took place in those heady days of the 90's when corporate excesses were arguably at their height. It certainly wasn't a daily occurrence and it wasn't exactly oligarch level bribery but there were a number of occasions when

when along with other colleagues I enjoyed some examples of corporate hospitality. These ranged from the enjoyable to the frankly surreal.

One of the strangest was a day at a seminar/ workshop at the premises of the Magic Circle in Euston, north London and the spiritual home of magicians in the UK. I don't remember the purpose of the day but it may have been one of the periodic exchanges of the strategic planning society. The venue looked like a large terraced building at the entrance but after coffees in a reception room with autographed and framed photos of famous practitioners including a case containing one of Tommy Cooper's fez's were were shown into a theatre at the back of the building the size of which seemed too large to for the buildings facade -magical!

I researching the book I found that Google earth doesn't provide images of the building in Stephenson's Way - mysterious.

Sporting events were often part of corporate entertaining and at the time I had limited interest in top level sports so usually gave and tickets to grateful colleagues. I did attend a home match at 'the Arsenal ground' and found it noisy and crowded with warm beer and a chewy pie. Similarly a one day Sussex cricket match was improved by the catering in the marquee away from the sunshine. The quality of catering at visits to the Hampton Court flower show and Royal Ascot was an improvement but at the racecourse the private box appeared like a beach hut with a small crowded veranda and the actual horse racing anticlimactic.

We did enjoy view events at Royal academy summer shows and some other art galleries.

Also there were some pleasant restaurant meals including a memorable visit to Raymond Blanc's Manoire de Quatre Saisons.

Two events I do remember were a two day creativity workshop run by Edward de Bono the acclaimed creative thinker and proponent of 'lateral thinking,' and secondly a seminar by Tom Peters. Both of these were highly regarded management gurus at the time and interesting to hear first hand.

Returning to the bizarre, one year we attended the National Utility Awards, held I think in London's Grosvener Hotel. Any time I see the BAFTA awards or similar ceremonies it comes back to mind as these events are formulaic with numerous round tables populated with dressed up people drinking the wine supplied and eating lukewarm salmon or chicken dishes. A 'celebrity' hosts would tell lame jokes, in our case it was cricketer David Gower and the various prize winners are called to collect eccentric looking trophies. Winning tables go crazy with excitement having been selected as 'new mapping software of the year,' or - and this is true 'the UK's best Trench contractor.' If that wasn't enough I recall my wife and another guest who was the dentist wife of a colleague dissolving into unruly hysterics at the finale of a mismatched (in height and girth) Scottish pipe band who were closing the proceedings.
Still at least I can say I have attended a national awards ceremony but I think I passed on the event in subsequent years.

Working in any large organisation to survive and be happy the individual must be prepared for and adapt to change because they will happen anyway. Sometimes they may be predictable or at least in part and other times they will just come out of the blue and be a shock.
In my career at Seeboard the changes that I anticipated included:-

The rationalisation of districts, I was working in one of the smallest in Sutton, and the merger was predictable because it had happened before.

The reduction in central processing and a move away from the dominant mainframe computer to dispersed intelligent local computing.

Privatisation, as this was well signalled in advance.

The slimming down of a large corporate head office and the development of more autonomous business units.

Maybe I didn't always anticipate them but being part of teams that were implementing them served to blur my memory.

During my career there were a few things that came a bit out of left field to me and I would include in this the move back to head office before privatisation, my assignment with reviewing Sussex TEC, my secondment to SEEDA and finally my role in selling the company.

Recent horrendous increases in energy prices for customers have led to a crisis of conscience as to what has happened to the industry that I spend my working life in. In my defence I state that I believed that my time there was spent on the whole morally and that along with my colleagues we worked hard to

220

maintain supplies and serve the needs of customers and latterly balancing this with decent returns to shareholders which in the case of most utilities in large include pension funds benefitting large numbers of the population.

So what has gone wrong ?

I believe that at the outset privatisation was a good thing and spurred efficiencies and innovation. At the same time this process was in some cases unhelpful in allowing ownership changes that increased short-term pursuits of profits.
Unfortunately the fragmentation of the industry reduced more strategic investment that had been possible in the earlier structure with the monolithic CEGB and the UK's atomic energy industry.
I remain to be convinced whether the industry regulator, Ofgem, has really done as much to help the situation.
The linkage of electricity to the wholesale price of gas also has escalated the exceptional price rises that we are currently experiencing.

Retirement

For most people in work, particularly those employed in companies and large organisations there is the end game of retirement. I realise for self employed people running their own businesses the situation is more complex and after I retired I realised that some of the envy I had felt for the apparent freedom of friends running their own businesses was illusory and also for them retirement or exiting the business was even more problematic. For me the end date was to some extent dictated by a number of factors. My pension scheme allowed me to reach my full entitlement after thirty years service which I achieved in my early fifties. The programmes that the company had been following for some time of restructuring and office closures relied on a policy of voluntary redundancies and early retirements particularly for senior staff to make way for younger employees to be promoted. Consequently a number of contemporaries had retired in their fifties and this option did not seem unattractive to me. There had also been a verbal understanding with the board of directors that once I completed a key task in the sale process of the company for them and the US owners then early retirement could be discussed and arranged.

It was a strange time during the transition. The new owners, EDF of France already owned London Electricity so the next few months were one of transition to merge the their two UK based companies. I had a limited involvement in the merger process but avoided any interviews for positions in the new organisation and strongly maintained my preference for retirement. There were a few awkward conversations about a temporary role in the integration process but this would be based in north London and more than double my daily commute which already took me two hours each day. Fortunately, the prior arrangement made with the previous board of directors was honoured and after a few months I found myself saying goodbye to colleagues and entering the next phase of my life. There were a few farewell lunches and the usual conversations along the lines of -'we cant believe you are leaving - you've always been here!'

I had one amusing final triumph over my final xmas. In recent years there had always been something of an informal competition over who received the best invite for lunch or dinner from business contacts; these were usually invites to nice restaurants in town or Brighton. Early in December I had a conversation with one of the directors of ESB, the Irish Electricity company that I had worked with to set up our Overseas Consultancy joint venture a few years previously. Donal asked about my future with EDF and was surprised that I was planning to retire and thought I was too young but we agreed that we would try and meet for lunch again before too long. As he often passed through London on business I assumed that would be where we'd meet. To my surprise a few days later I received a good luck card from Donal together with a business class BA return ticket to Dublin for the week before xmas.

I rang Donal and he said if the date wasn't convenient he could change it but if it was he would see me in Dublin for lunch!

The trip was very enjoyable starting with an early breakfast in the business lounge at Gatwick followed by the short flight to Dublin on a clear day enlivened by recognising landmarks in my home town as we flew down the Bristol Channel, spacious seats and the company of an Irish priest sitting next to me drinking large whiskies for reassurance as well as crossing himself on landing.

Donal had arranged a car to collect me at the airport and after coffees in the ESB we went off to a nice city restaurant for a lavish lunch. Over lunch he asked me whether I would be interested in some consultancy work with them once I had retired, initially in Poland.

223

This was a surprise and I think it was partially the reason for the invite. I said I would think about it but didn't yet have a firm retirement date so maybe it was a bit premature.

There was time for some quick xmas shopping in Grafton Street before heading back to the airport for a late afternoon flight.

I didn't follow up the opportunity with ESB in Eastern Europe but my story of xmas lunch and shopping in Dublin was seen as the pinnacle of seasonal hospitality back at the office.

After so long with the company the actual leaving was very low key as many in our head office were uncertain of their futures and it seemed a little unfair of me to be too jubilant about securing my preferred outcome. I summed up the situation as me handing back the keys to the company Mercedes, their lap-top and mobile phone and receiving my life back or 'they used to pay me to come here and now I am being paid not to come here!'

What happened next ?

One of the first things people do in retirement is to set about all those tasks that they have been too busy to complete whilst working. I had a few of these including an 18th century house that always needed some attention, similar demands from two old classic cars and a garden of several acres that we had allegedly created from a field to be 'low maintenance,' but the tall hedges and lush planting as well as the mowing seemed to belie this claim. The good news was that my wife and our last remaining dog, an energetic collie cross, both seemed happy to spend more time with me and the feeling was mutual.

Shortly after retiring the opportunity came up to buy a modest holiday home in an area we had been going to for a number of years. In 'Small House in Crete' published on Amazon, I tell the story of this as well as our enrolment, at home in Sussex, in a Greek school for weekly classes in an attempt to at least acquire some greek language skills. The most beneficial part of this was being thrown into a Greek environment for the two hour class which was the usual southern European form of organised, friendly chaos. Pupils and their parents, as the majority of the class were children, would arrive and depart at random times in the two hour lesson slot. The classes were held in the church hall attached to a Victorian church now converted by the Cypriot community to a Greek orthodox church, complete with icons and incense burners so there were also the occasional appearances of the Greek orthodox priest who would bless the class at the start and end of term and also appear on saint or name days. This was usually accompanied by the sprinkling of holy water using the traditional bunches of basil sprigs. Not a welcome ordeal for some of the teenage girls who had already prepared for the weekend with routines of hair washing and straightening. Initially the lesson were provided by one of the church elders, Mr Bouras, and the textbooks used were Greek junior school books of a 'Janet and John' genre. The children in the stories were supplemented by Disney characters so we found ourselves learning to read, write and speak, "Goofy would like to play bat and ball." Not really the vocabulary that I could see being useful. Now if Goofy wants to buy a full tank of unleaded for his hire car we may be making progress. That would probably be covered in later lesson. Classes in the years following the first one were taken by Greek students who the Greek Ministry of Culture would pay for and it allowed them to earn money whilst studying. The three that taught us over the years were all mature students in

225

their thirties and qualified teachers. Mr Bouras was rather territorial over the teaching and insisted that they spend a number of weeks 'observing his teaching before being allowed to 'teach solo' which must have been somewhat frustrating for them. Eventually they took over although I quite liked Mr Bouras teaching us as we used to have lengthy digressions over the origins of Greek words and their incorporation into the English language. I genuinely found this helped me to remember the vocabulary although the other students enjoyed catching up on gossip whilst this took place. It also put off the dreaded marking of the homework - yes we had homework set!

The other unexpected bonus from the Greek class was my re-entry into the art world which I had left around the age of fifteen when choosing GCE O level subjects. My red brick grammar school didn't consider Art to be a useful academic subject so I had reluctantly been persuaded to drop art at GCE O level in favour of the more prestigious Latin or Additional Maths!
On the drive home after Greek school we passed a double fronted ground floor gallery that always looked busy with a crowd of people chatting and holding wine glasses. We recognised that it must be a private view evening but were intrigued that it seemed to be a weekly event. One week our curiosity got the better of us and we called in. That evening I could tell the framed art on the wall was the work of several different artists and through the crowded room we made our way to the reception desk where we were welcomed and asked to sign in to be put on their mailing list and given a form to sign up to become members of what we discovered was the 'Hastings Arts Forum.' We could be guests for that evening and were encouraged to help ourselves to a glass of wine each, provided by the exhibitors. This all seemed very hospitable. As we looked at the art on the walls through the crowded room a smiling man asked us if

we liked the work in what I easily recognised was a Scottish accent. We said we did and asked if any of it was his work and when he modestly showed us some beautiful coloured portraits that he described as mono prints, a term I was unfamiliar with but was known to my wife, her education and background having followed a much more artistic path than I had. My enquiry to George, as we were to discover he was called, whether he had always been a professional artist was met with laughter - "Oh no, I had a career in IT - I only started this a couple of years ago. A number of us here attend a weekly print class here at Hastings College. Come along this Friday, I'll arrange for you to see what we do and later perhaps arrange a trial free session - it's very relaxed." I looked again at the rich colours of the framed art and George's smiling face and thought why not.

Friday found me a little less confident as I drove to Hastings but George was very friendly and what did I have to lose, I could always say it wasn't for me.The Art College was just above the seafront, housed in what seemed to be the basement of a Victorian building, although once inside there was natural light to towards the sea where the ground sloped down. There were some dozen 'artists' of mixed ages and George welcomed me wearing a paint stained apron saying it's best not to dress up for printing. He introduced me to the tutor and then gave me a tour of the studio. There were printing beds for the silk screens, drying racks, rows of tables, a huge light box like a jumbo photocopier and a wet-room for spray cleaning the screens. He explained the process for producing silk screen prints from photos which was a technique that interested me more than mono printing which looks to be a more skilful technique and explained that Ian the tutor would explain what I would need for next week to produce my own image. After an initial trial session I signed up for the full term a couple of weeks later. A few months later I had sold the first two limited edition prints at an event in a restaurant in Lewes much to my surprise and pleasure. Within a year I had joined a group of several other printers for the first group exhibition. To our relief we all sold work and it more than recovered the large wine bill that made for a memorable evening. My work was mostly using photographs taken in Sussex and Crete and digitally working on them on a Mac before creating the image sets to transfer to screens. Images photographed in the villages on the island comprised some of my early prints with doors and windows offering easy photogenic subjects.

I enjoyed the mix of creating hand printed silkscreen from digital photos. I also tried some etching and mono printing but wasn't ever truly satisfied with the results. I carried on printing for several more years at the college and made some great friends there. All arising from stopping in a gallery one night. So many thanks George for inspiring me, your art is still more accomplished than mine is but it's not a competition. I was very grateful to tutors Ian, Myles and Jackie as well as learning from other colleagues on the course especially George Mundell, Del Querns and Andy Smith who is a successful and well known commercial artist and printer.

Contact there led to another new experience when fellow printer Del set up a new business with his business partner Richard - a record shop and who of my generation hasn't wanted to work in a record shop! I recommend 'Music's Not Dead' to music fans. At that time Del and Rich had taken a lease on a premises in Bexhill town that was previously a cafe. They were going for a cheap and cheerful makeover before an early opening to sell cd's and vinyl. I offered to help and a week of cleaning and painting followed before a carpenter came in to create the shelving racks and a counter. After the opening I spent the odd day serving there to help out when Rich was off. It was an interesting experience and great to reminisce with customers about favourite albums and bands we had seen. Many customers were buying back catalogue items and it was amusing to see awe struck younger customers reaction to hearing that you had seen the Doors or Hendrix live. A nice nostalgic experience - though hard work I am sure as a business. The business has developed, extending the range of vinyl and putting on live events as well as a

229

mail order business. It has become a destination for musos from all over the south of England and further. The shop has since moved into the Art Deco seafront De la Warr pavilion making it, I would contend, the only grade 1 listed record shop in existence. As a result of our house move I can only visit occasionally and my several Saturdays working in the music business are just another happy memory.

The other avenue that the house in Crete opened up to me was what is happening here on the page. We spend a lifetime writing as students, corresponding by letter and latterly by emails and text. Some of us also apply this skill in our work to a greater or lesser extent but it's common for people to muse - 'I could wrote a book on that.' The experience of finding, buying and renovating the house in Crete made me think that I had material that was interesting enough to write down and just maybe others would find the content interesting enough to read. Advances in desk top publishing and the use of the internet to publish, market and distribute have all made this possible.

I did briefly experiment with re-entering the world of work via the popular route of consultancy. I had seen an advert somewhere for experienced professionals to join a small consultancy specialising in coaching and change management using short term contracts. Some weeks after sending off my CV I was invited to an interview day in a hotel near Birmingham where several dozen other applicants had also been invited. We were given details about the consultancy who were based on the Welsh border but operated nationally. Their approach was described to us and we were told that there would be a series of induction days for us to learn their prescribed approach before we would be involved in any chargeable assignments. A few days later I was phoned and asked if I was still interested and would I be willing to attend the first induction day at their offices. As I was not sure about being fully retired in my mid-fifties I agreed to attend.

A group of ten prospective consultants attended the first induction day which was described as free of charge but we were to pay for our own travel and any necessary accommodation for the days. Our backgrounds varied; a couple of us were newly retired from industry others had come from careers in education or local authorities. The approach of the consultancy appeared sensible and practical with most of the current and planned client base being in the fields of education or local government. There was talk of NLP (neuro-linguistic programming,) and other jargon laden management speak but once I had stripped away the jargon I recognised much of it as sensible change management processes. I agreed to attend a further session before committing to any contractual arrangements.

In the event after several more training days I only worked on three short term assignments of a day or two day duration during the next few months. Apart from one assignment in east London the other two were in the Midlands and the North of England and the travel and tax implications of such as a small amount of work had me questioning whether this was something that I would persevere with. I must admit the structured training gave me an idea that I could apply my experience from my career together with this as an independent coach/mentor and since retirement I have undertaken a few assignments as such, some paid, some pro bono and I have enjoyed all of them.

One took place over a longer period and included an ascent to the top of Nelson's Column in Trafalgar Square where the company was undertaking a stone restoration project, this was somewhere I never thought I would find myself and I'm not over keen on heights! But thank you Adrian for the experience.

The same assignment found me running a business planning session at the IOD (the Institute of Directors,) in Pall Mall where to my astonishment an

old school and university friend, Vernon, was one of
the board members there. This led later to a very
convivial lunch and catch up after a gap of some
decades.

Socialising after a working life can also lead to
unexpected events. As my office was almost an hour's
drive away and fellow inmates could be commuting
from another direction it was unlikely that after work
you would socialise easily unless it was prearranged.
Some of this became possible in retirement with the
establishment of regular 'pub lunch' meetings
arranged by emails but an amusing event took place
at a more formally arranged meeting.
We were invited to lunch in the next town by a retired
colleague and his wife, along with another couple we
knew, the husband was also a fellow retiree and a bit
of a stickler for formality We had already met as a
group having an informal 'kitchen supper,' at our
house a few weeks before. To preserve anonymity and
avoid any further embarrassment I will omit any
names but the lady host had 'pushed the boat out'
with lunch arranged in the large formal dining room
with the table laid out with best dinner service, cutlery
and an array of expensive crystal glassware. After a
pre lunch drink we took our seats to eat the first
course when my fellow guest suddenly lurched to one

side as his dining chair gave way under him. There was no real damage apart from pride and the chair. The host expressed surprise and started a forensic examination of the chair which didn't surprise me as he had been one of the company's more cerebral employees with a clutch of qualifications and a national reputation for developing complex mathematical models. The hostess was less impressed and pressed her husband to remove the offending item and and bring another chair. Reluctantly he did so whilst speculating on the damaging effects of modern heating systems on pre-twentieth century family heirlooms. Lunch recommenced but the restored fragile peace was soon interrupted by a second collapsing chair, this time to the partner of the first victim. The wooden culprit was more speedily replaced on this occasion but the lunch party nervously sat out the next three courses and I avoided second offerings of any of the heavier foods available and ate less than my usual helping of the cheese and biscuits. Coffee was served in the sitting room on substantial sofas much to the relief of everyone. The journey home was quiet until after we were dropped of in our drive and the car with the erstwhile furniture vandals had driven off when both of degenerated into hysterical laughter. I soon recovered although Stephanie only had to say 'the chairs' for her hysterics to return - and this went on for several days even though I mentioned that the joke, rather like the chair frames, was wearing a bit thin.

Strangely, the damaging couple didn't invite the four of us to their house for a return meal perhaps fearing some damaging reprisals and in the years since the incident hasn't been a topic of conversation....until now!

In 2013 after a quarter of a century in our Sussex country cottage we took the decision that the rural idyll no longer suited us. We still wanted to travel more; longer stays in the holiday home in Crete had us virtually hacking our way up the garden path on our return and driving miles to shop for even a bottle of milk was losing any appeal it may have had. We remembered living in town in Worthing and the ease with which we could do things locally and it held a new attraction to us. We were conscious that the two acre garden that we had created from a field in our time there was becoming more of a maintenance than a creative activity and although we would miss it we weren't afraid of making big changes in our life.

Now that we had decided we wanted to move the big question was 'where would we move to?' Hastings town on the Sussex coast had provided us both with Greek classes at the Greek church there, I had attended the Art college for printmaking for a couple of years. We occasionally visited Rye for shopping and days out, likewise Brighton that offered shopping and entertainment at arts venues. Bexhill on Sea was also briefly considered and dismissed. It was my wife who said one day -'what about Swansea,' my home town. I believe my reply was along the lines of me leaving there a long time ago and never thinking I would return to live there. As we talked about it I realised that it fitted many of the criteria we had been mentally listing: big enough to have a variety of things going on; countryside nearby; a range of housing types; it was known to us; a university etc. My one reservation was the lack of a nearby airport but we found limited flights to Crete from Bristol airport and other destinations from Cardiff.

Although I no longer work I am always interested in a brief discussion with a business owner when in a shop, cafe or restaurant and still find that I like to find out how things work for them such as marketing via social media, or seasonal changes for their business.

Once in Swansea my thoughts turned again to finding new activities

Environment Centre

This was a charitable organisation supported by the city   council in an in interesting building within walking distance   along the key side of our new home.
  I called in there to see what volunteering opportunities they   had and the manager told me they were looking for people   to take on half day shifts in their shop/coffee shop. I was also asked whether I had any sales experience. In answering I judged it wise not to mention my role in the   sale of the energy company for 1.5 billion pounds that was   now paying my pension or my teenage   holidays selling   knitwear but instead mentioned helping recently in my friends record shop. This seemed the right answer and it   was suggested   that I came in one morning for a training   session before 'flying solo.'
  At this session later in the week I was introduced to the mysteries off the stockroom, the coffee machine, phone and the till all of which I felt I could manage. The following Thursday morning I was temporary manager of the Environment Centre shop and coffee bar!
  I had initially been attracted by the building itself as it was the original telephone exchange for the docks, an impressive brick building with a modern environmentally friendly extension which I had been impressed with.
  The shop and cafe were in the modern extension with a mezzanine level upstairs for meetings. In other parts of the original building the full-time staff were involved in grant funded projects of an environmental nature. For several months I had my weekly morning stint in the shop and gradually became more involved

in the organisation taking part in planning meetings and agreeing to take on a role as one of the trustees.

At the same time I had taken on a greater level of commitment at the Friends of the Copperworks group agreeing to act as temporary Chairmen to put the voluntary group on a more formal footing and develop relations with both the City Council and Swansea University.

The involvement ranged from organising meetings and agreeing a formal constitution to the more interesting activities such as guided walks and producing publicity and newsletters. The involvement was satisfying and I met some interesting and enthusiastic fellow volunteers. Commitments with the Copperworks meant I resigned the trusteeship and concentrated on the friends of the Copperworks group.

The other voluntary activity was as a River Ranger. I had heard about an initiative to record wildlife activity in the River Tawe, labelled as the River Ranger project so intrigued I made contact and attended the introductory meeting. The project came under some form of grant funding so to my surprise the group of some eight or ninnies individuals were issued with expensive GPS devices and a share in the funding, some £250 each to be spent on appropriate items such as binoculars and wet weather clothing.

The plan was that each 'ranger' would survey their allocated area of water at least several times a month or as frequently as possible and report sightings of interest such as migratory birds or incidents of pollution. There were several half day trips to view different sections of the Tawe with explanations about flood plains, erosion, invasive bankside species and polluting discharges and drainage issues.

At my request I was allocated the lower basin of the river Tawe, within walking distance of our house and for a couple of months diligently completed monthly reports, complete with photos. I saw and reported the adult seal that fishes below the fish ladder at the rivers

237

mouth and identified Turnstones, small speckled birds that I had not been aware of before. The involvement opened my eyes to nature in post-industrial landscape

close to the city centre that was now our new home. Unfortunately, the initiative came to a premature close at the end of the first year when funds were not renewed for the co-ordinator and there was no replacement to send reports to. It made me aware of the vulnerability of these kind of funded project, still on a positive note I still have the binoculars and I know what a turnstone looks like!

Another interesting diversion for me in retirement, particularly having moved to a city, was having the time to take an interest in local developments. We now live in a new house built on a maritime development close to the city in a dock lands setting comprising a mixture of business and leisure as well as residential. I had heard that a new a SA1 (the name given by the city to the development,) Business Club was starting and had invited people who lived and worked in the area to a monthly meeting in a hotel with a buffet lunch. Now in retirement after a corporate life a 'free lunch' is a rarity and not too be sniffed at! The meetings are always interesting and it's been a good way to hear about developments in the city and to meet some of the people making this happen. It was also a useful forum to promote the Copperworks friends activities to. It was here that I first heard about the plans for the new city arena and park, now built. The UWTSD campus in the dock lands, also built. The plans for the Skyline project and Lagoon; still being developed as well as other schemes and proposals.

Several years on I have yet to be asked what my business is in SA1 and have even taken along some guests who were amused when the organisers greet me by name. I did find a productive thing to do through the business club when I heard that UWTSD were running a kind of 'Dragon's Den' initiative called a Race to Market. This was a week in their final term where aspiring students could develop and pitch their business ideas to grant funds and potential investors. The university was asking for volunteer mentors to coach and rehearse the pitches during the week before their final presentations. I enjoyed working with the students and they appeared to welcome my comments. There were a broad range of business ideas presented from fitness training programmes to assisted limb technologies. My role there must have been seen to add some value as I was pleased to be asked to participate at the following year's event. A new revelation was made to me when I was asked to approve my description in the publicity for the week and was told they were repeating the text they had used for me the previous year. To my surprise it included the phrase -"Geoff Dendle, an eminent economist." Unbeknown to me I had been 'eminent' for at least twelve months ! Who would have thought that?

The role as chairman of the Friends of Hafod and Morfa Copperworks was to gradually develop into an almost part-time job and eventually occupied more of my time than was sensible. It began with my attendance at a training session for tour guides to show members of the public around a site of Swansea's copper industry on the banks of the river Tawe. It wasn't my first involvement there. In the 1960's there was a large scale environmental project to clean up the area including replanting trees at the site, up the slopes of Kilvey hill. The sulphurous fumes from over a century of heavy industry had decimated the area of any vegetation. Our school was involved and one afternoon a coachload of us as fresh faced schoolboys were found on the bleak slope planting small native tree saplings. It must have succeeded as the same slopes today are heavily wooded.

A few years later our history class were asked whether any of us would like to participate as volunteers on an archeology dig being carried out by the university on Kilvey hill. There was speculation about the possibility of a Roman hill fort at the site so it was with some degree of excitement after a few hours of careful scratching away in a trench that we exposed the white edge of what looked like a bone. One of the supervising staff were called over and as it was near the end of the day some covers were put over the trench and we were told we would find out more the following weekend.

We returned the following Saturday to be met with stony faced staff and students who had spent the previous week painstakingly excavating a recent horse carcass. Our enquiry whether it might have been Roman didn't seem to cheer them up. I think that was my one and only planned involvement in amateur archaeology.

The Copperworks friends group expanded their activities with amongst other things a regular programme of guided tours for the public as well as prearranged groups such as schools and historical societies. Dialogues with the city council and Swansea university continued and input to funding applications was often sought by both as evidence of wider community involvement. One such funding grant resulted in the removal and refurbishment of a travelling crane from the roof of one of the engine houses as part of the restoration of the building. The friends group organised the removal and complete restoration of the crane in a local workshop owned by Tom Henderson, an enthusiastic engineer member of the friends. But I was finding the process of dealing with large organisations such as the city council and the university increasingly frustrating. As a voluntary organisation I often felt we were being used when it was convenient to show community involvement in bids or for public relations purposes and could see my energy for the group waning.

We arranged the donation of a porta cabin from a local construction company, (thank you Griffiths.) Successfully crowd sourced funds to fit it out as well as winning another funding bid for publicity materials but the frustrations continued with the council and CADW the heritage organisation raising planning difficulties over siting the cabin which was to provide a useful on-site presence for the Friends group. After the country shut down with the pandemic restrictions I felt ready to relinquish the chairmanship of the group and let others

develop it. The group continues and the guided tours are more popular than ever which I am pleased about. I am welcomed at the friends meetings but I am

241

currently happy with a role as an interested observer. It is pleasing that post the pandemic the group has become active again with an enthusiastic committee running a programme of events. It will be pleasing to see further progress at the site.

I have continued with my writings and this latest book will be the eleventh title of my narrative and photo journal books published on Amazon books. Some of these are photos collected travelling which retirement gives you more freedom for.
I hope it demonstrates that work can be fun and there is more to life than work.

Returning to Aberystwyth

Printed in Great Britain
by Amazon

25191595R00137